MARY AND JOHN GRIBBIN

Inventing the FUTURE

Illustrated by
Mark Oliver

PUFFIN

contents

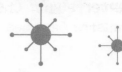

PUFFIN BOOKS

For Jon and Ben, with love and thanks

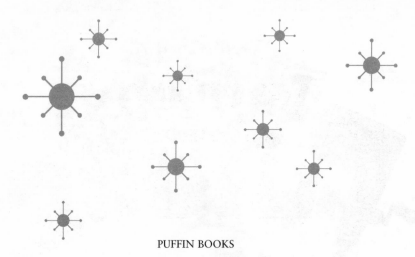

PUFFIN BOOKS

Published by the Penguin Group
Penguin Books Ltd, 80 Strand, London WC2R 0RL, England
Penguin Group (USA), Inc., 375 Hudson Street, New York, New York 10014, USA
Penguin Books Australia Ltd, 250 Camberwell Road, Camberwell, Victoria 3124, Australia
Penguin Books Canada Ltd, 10 Alcorn Avenue, Toronto, Ontario, Canada M4V 3B2
Penguin Books India (P) Ltd, 11 Community Centre, Panchsheel Park, New Delhi – 110 017, India
Penguin Group (NZ), cnr Airborne and Rosedale Roads, Albany, Auckland 1310, New Zealand
Penguin Books (South Africa) (Pty) Ltd, 24 Sturdee Avenue, Rosebank 2196, South Africa

Penguin Books Ltd, Registered Offices: 80 Strand, London WC2R 0RL, England

www.penguin.com

First published 2004
1

Text copyright © John and Mary Gribbin, 2004
Illustrations copyright © Mark Oliver, 2004
All rights reserved

The moral right of the authors and illustrator has been asserted

Made and printed in England by Clays Ltd, St Ives plc

British Library Cataloguing in Publication Data
A CIP catalogue record for this book is available from the British Library

ISBN 0–670–91502–5

From Aristotle to Atoms

This is a book about people who happened to be scientists, not a book about science itself. We wrote it because those people had interesting lives and because lots of them did other things besides being scientists. For example, Sir Isaac Newton, the most famous scientist of them all, wasn't knighted for his science, but for something else entirely – and he gave up science at the age of forty-four to do something completely different. (If you want to know what, you'll have to read the book.) He was also an unpleasant, bad-tempered man, who couldn't bear it if anyone came up with a good idea before he did. And Charles Darwin wasn't the only person who came up with the idea of evolution by natural selection. Another man, just as clever as Darwin, had the same idea, even though most people have never heard of him.

It's also interesting that somebody else came up with the same idea as Darwin at about the same time. The way the story of science is often told, it is easy to get the impression that all the important discoveries were made by geniuses, who had amazing intelligence and ability. But that isn't so. Science actually progresses step by step, with each new contribution building on top of what has gone before, like building a house from the ground up. People like Newton and Darwin were very clever, but not really any cleverer than a lot of other people around at the time. They added their knowledge to what had gone before, as other clever people alive at the time did. For example, some of Newton's most famous theories were first suggested by a man named Robert Hooke. And some of Charles Darwin's ideas were actually thought of by his grandfather, Erasmus Darwin.

You don't have to be a rare genius to be a good scientist; all you need is to have a good and questioning brain, and to understand the science that has gone before.

We don't have room to tell you about all the interesting scientists who ever lived, but we've picked out some of our favourites, many of whom had interesting lives. Of course, we can't tell you about them without mentioning a bit of science, so we've tried to put the stories together to show how the scientific understanding of the world developed, brick by brick, from the time of the Ancient Greek philosopher Aristotle, right up to the discovery of atoms.

There's one kind of person you will rarely meet in this book, though. Until recently, women weren't allowed to go to university and they weren't expected to do things like science at all. Now we know that women are just as clever as men and there have been many female scientists in the past hundred years or so. Some of them have won the Nobel Prize, the top award in science. But their story comes after the story we have to tell, which is about the earlier days of science.

The people you will meet along the way include a doctor who discovered how the heart works and once sat under a hedge during a battle, reading a book while cannonballs whistled past; a millionaire scientist who was so shy he would run away if he ever met a woman; and a man whose first scientific job was washing out test tubes, but who became the greatest British scientist of his generation. We hope you enjoy meeting them as much as we have.

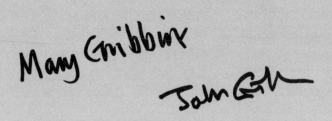

chapter one

BIG
Ideas

Big Ideas

Over the past 2,000 years our knowledge of the universe has grown from virtually nothing to the vast amount we know today. But humans have been around for more than two million years. So why wasn't science invented sooner?

Early people didn't have time to sit around thinking because of all the effort that they had to put in just to stay alive. Finding food and shelter, looking after their families and keeping everyone safe from murderous neighbours and wild animals took up almost every moment. Living in constant fear of starvation and always on the alert in case of attack left very little time for deep thought about the world and how it works.

Settling down

As time moved on, people became more secure by living together in large groups within settled communities. Farming was more successful than hunting because people didn't have to chase after game for food, but could stay in one place and farm the land together. As these communities became more successful they grew richer and larger until they developed into towns and cities. People were able to specialize in what they did best: the best hunters hunted, the best farmers farmed and the best metalworkers made weapons, plates and cups for eating and drinking.

There was enough food, shelter and clothing to allow the richest and most powerful people to pay for those with skills to make jewellery, music, art objects and good clothes; to teach, entertain, cure the sick and work out ways to improve life.

Towns and cities had powerful leaders who often had to struggle to maintain their power and look after their people. These leaders started to surround themselves with the most intelligent people they could find to help them to work out problems and to give them advice. At last some people had the time to think. Thinking became valued, knowledge became power and communities developed into civilizations.

The word 'philosophy' comes from the Greek word philosophia, which means 'lover of wisdom'.

The Greeks get going

The first real thinking was done in the time of the Ancient Greeks. In Greek society all the hard work was done by slaves, who were forced to spend their lives looking after their owners' houses and land. This was very tough on the slaves but it meant that the people they served had enough time to come up with ideas about the way the world works, and could enjoy such things as poetry and science. Science in Ancient Greece was thought of as philosophy.

Rich people who didn't have the talent themselves paid poets and philosophers to do the thinking and creating for them. They gave them money and food to put on plays or to teach them about the world. In a way, these philosophers were entertainers, rather like the makers of TV documentaries today.

Studying the stars

We know that even before the Greeks there had been people who studied or did things we would now call science. But they did them mostly for very practical reasons (or because the king or a priest told them to). Astronomy is often called the first science, because we know that people studied the patterns made by the stars on the sky (the constellations) at least 5,000 years ago. They studied these patterns because the way the appearance of the night sky changes during the year is related to the pattern of the seasons on Earth, and this helped farmers know when was the best time to plant their crops.

This is probably the reason why Stonehenge, on Salisbury Plain in England, was built. Stonehenge is made of several rings of stones and other constructions. The stones are lined up with special astronomical events, like the places on the horizon where the Sun sets and rises at certain times of the year, so we know the people who built it were interested in astronomy. Whoever ordered it to be built must have been rich, powerful and very well organized, or they wouldn't have been able to feed all the workers involved.

The big questions

Until about 600 BC what we now know as mathematics, medicine and astronomy had been studied simply because they were useful and enabled people to solve practical problems. It wasn't until the Ancient Greeks came along that science began to be something people did out of interest, and for fun.

Greek science was mostly about thinking, and not very much about doing. The Greek philosophers were very good at asking big questions, like 'What is everything made of?' and 'How do things move?' and 'Did the Universe have a beginning?' But they didn't try to solve them practically; the way they tried to answer these questions was simply by looking at the world around them and thinking deeply about it.

Archimedes

A brilliant man of ideas – famous for shouting 'Eureka!' during a brainwave – his achievements rival those of people who lived more than 1,000 years later.

The most well-known story about Archimedes is how he solved the puzzling problem of why an object seems to get lighter as you lower it into water. He was sitting in his bath one day, thinking, and suddenly worked out the answer – at which he got so excited that he leapt out of the bath and ran out naked into the streets, shouting, '*Eureka!*'

'Eureka' means 'I've got it!' in Ancient Greek.

Archimedes had discovered one of the fundamental laws of physics, which is still called Archimedes' principle. Thinking about his body lying in the bath had given him the answer to the problem: he realized that things seem lighter when they are lowered into water because the water pushes against the object and supports some of its weight.

We now know this as 'upthrust' and it is always equal to the weight of the water that the object pushes away as it drops into the water. An object will float if the upthrust is more than its weight but it will sink if its weight is heavier than the upthrust.

Archimedes' principle ('upthrust') is vital to the design of ships and submarines because the designer needs to work out exactly how deep a ship will lie in the water.

The young boy

Archimedes lived in the town of Stagira, Greece, for most

It's strange that the most famous story about Archimedes takes place in a bath – as washing was not his favourite pastime . . .

of his life (287–212 BC). From an early age maths was his greatest love. When he was a young man he had been lucky enough to study with the greatest mathematicians in the known world, who had all gathered in Alexandria, in Egypt.

Dirty work

As an adult Archimedes remained completely obsessed by his mathematical work and would often get so deeply into it that he would forget to wash for days on end. Plutarch, a Greek historian, described in his writings how Archimedes would have to be dragged down to the baths by his servants to get him cleaned up. Even while he was in the baths he would try to keep on with his calculations by writing on his own body or in the soot surrounding the bathhouse chimneys. This obsession with maths would eventually be the cause of his death.

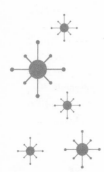

The Romans are coming!

In 212 BC, Marcellus, a Roman general, laid siege to the Greek city of Syracuse. The Romans were kept at bay for many months by the Greeks, who used some impressive war machines to defend themselves. Many of these were designed by Archimedes himself, including a spectacular giant catapult that fired large rocks at the Roman soldiers and ships. Another invention was Archimedes' claw, a massive lever with a hook attached that was hidden behind the sea wall. When an enemy ship came close, the machine was swung round to 'hook' the ship like a giant fish and upturn it in the water.

There are stories that Archimedes also invented a system of mirrors to focus the Sun's rays on to enemy ships, setting fire to them.

Despite these skilful defences, the Romans eventually breached the city and invaded. Killing and looting as they went, they surged forward into the city, a victorious army eager to conquer the city that had held out against them for so long.

too wrapped up for war

But Archimedes had no idea that his city was being invaded. He was so involved with his work that he paid no attention to the terrible noises around him. Ignoring the world, he continued to work out a geometrical problem by drawing circles in the dust around his feet.

As Archimedes was bending over his drawings, a Roman soldier rushed up to him brandishing a sword, and demanded to know his name. Archimedes tried to protect his dusty drawings and shouted out, 'I beg you, don't disturb this!' This enraged the soldier so much that he slaughtered Archimedes on the spot.

The historian Livy, writing in his history of Rome around the time that Christ was born, said, 'It is on record that Archimedes, while intent upon figures which he had traced in the dust, and regardless of the hideous roar of the army let loose to ravage and despoil a captured city, was killed by a soldier who did not know who he was.'

Marcellus organized a funeral for Archimedes and tried to make amends by seeking out his family and treating them well in order to pay honour to his memory.

A regretful Roman

When Marcellus found out that one of his own soldiers had hacked Archimedes down in cold blood, he was devastated. Even though his invasion plans had long been thwarted by Archimedes' defences for the city, Marcellus had great respect for the man and had wanted to meet him.

To his dying day, he deeply regretted the murder. The historian Plutarch wrote that 'Nothing afflicted Marcellus so much as the death of Archimedes.'

Socrates, Plato and Aristotle

Philosophers like Aristotle often walked about while they were discussing their ideas. Aristotle's followers in particular became known as the 'Peripatetics', from the Greek word peripatētikos, which means 'walking up and down'.

The three most famous Greek philosophers. Outspoken Socrates – who was killed for speaking his mind – his loyal pupil Plato, and Aristotle, the most important of all the Greek philosophers in history.

Aristotle (384–322 BC) became so important because a lot of his scientific writing survived and was read by later generations. Even 1,700 years after he died, scholars in Europe called him *Ille Philosophus*: 'the master of them that know'. They believed every word he wrote (that didn't go against biblical teaching) as an eternal truth.

Words of Wisdom

Sophists would wander around the different city states, settling down for a time and passing on their knowledge.

In all the centuries from the time of the Ancient Greeks up to those European scholars, there were no printing presses or computers. Every word of every copy of every book had to be handwritten by a scribe, so books were precious and copies were rare. Very often, all the copies of a particular book ended up getting lost or destroyed. Just by chance, copies of Aristotle's books survived while most of the books written by other Greek philosophers have been lost. This is why almost everything we know about Ancient Greek science comes from Aristotle.

Cities of learning

Ancient Greece was divided into many city states that valued learning and set up academies, which were like schools or universities, with visiting scholars and teachers. The teachers were known as 'sophists', from the Greek word *sophistēs*, which means 'expert'.

At the academies, young men could learn about philosophy, mathematics and science while sitting or walking about in the olive groves. They also did sports, carrying on the Greek belief that physical exercise was just as important as mental exercise.

Socrates, who lived from 469 BC to 399 BC, was one of the great sophists. He was, by all accounts, a wonderful teacher but we only know about his ideas because they were written down by his famous pupil, Plato (who lived from about 428 BC to 348 BC).

Socrates speaks his mind

Socrates started out in life as a stonemason, but when his father, a successful sculptor called Sophroniscus, died, he inherited enough money to live the rest of his life without being paid for his teaching. This independence meant that Socrates could say and do as he saw fit. He encouraged his pupils – the rich aristocratic citizens of Athens – to question the truth of popular opinions, and he voiced his own opinions, whether or not they fitted in with the political rulers of the time. This did not go down well with those in power.

The drink of death

It took a long time but eventually Socrates' free-speaking got him into serious trouble. At the grand old age of eighty he was found guilty of 'neglect of the gods' and 'corrupting' the youth of Athens with

There were no girls in the academies, because in those days girls were only educated in the skills that would enable them to become good housekeepers and mothers. They were not allowed to take up careers outside the home.

Most of Plato's own writings were lost after his death, and copies of some of his books were only found hundreds of years later.

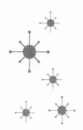

The hemlock plant is so poisonous that just a few drops of its juice can be fatal. The Ancient Greeks often used hemlock to put criminals to death.

his outspoken views. For this, he was condemned to death and made to drink a poison made from hemlock root. Socrates coped with death in the same philosophical way he had coped with life, and freely drank the hemlock while surrounded by his friends and supporters.

Plato, grief-stricken by Socrates' death, left Athens to live abroad for several years. This was a wise move; Greece had become a dangerous place for anyone who had been a friend of the great man.

Mighty Macedonia

The wars between the city states meant that Greece was going through a time of great change when Aristotle was a child. His connection with Macedonia would have an important bearing on the rest of his life.

Plato did return to Athens some years later. He set up his own academy in the city.

Aristotle's father had been a physician at the court of King Amyntas III, who ruled the city state of Macedonia. King Amyntas III died in 369 BC, and his son Philip II set about conquering his neighbours. By 339 BC Macedonia ruled the whole of Greece. While that had been going on, a young Aristotle had been studying at Plato's Academy in Athens. He did so well that he became one of the teachers, and stayed there for twenty years, until Plato died. Plato had left orders that his nephew should take over as head of the Academy, and Aristotle immediately left Athens. Historians don't know if he was annoyed at not being appointed head of the Academy, or if it was because anyone connected with the Macedonian rulers was unpopular in Athens at the time.

The young king

Whatever his reasons, Aristotle stayed away from Athens for twelve years, discussing philosophy with

other sophists and studying natural history. After a long stay on the island of Lesbos, in 342 BC he went back to Macedonia, where Philip II asked him to tutor his thirteen-year-old son, Alexander.

Alexander had a wonderful time with his inspirational new teacher. Aristotle taught him all about philosophy, zoology and botany. He also introduced him to the world of poetry and writing, giving him a copy of a famous book called Homer's *Illiad*. Alexander is said to have slept with a copy of this book under his pillow for the rest of his life. All in all, Aristotle was like a second father to the young man. As a man, Alexander often said that his father had given him life but Aristotle had given him the knowledge to live it well.

When he was forty-nine, in 335 BC, Aristotle at last returned to Athens. Alexander, who had just become king, encouraged him to set up his own academy, called the Lyceum. (Alexander probably paid for this himself.) After Alexander died in 323 BC, life in Athens once again became uncomfortable for anyone with a Macedonian connection. Aristotle retired to the island of Euboea, where he died the following year, but his legacy was to be influential right up to modern times.

The essential elements

According to Aristotle, the Greeks thought that everything on Earth was made up of a combination of four elements: fire, earth, air and water. In the same way, the properties of everything on Earth were explained by combining four attributes: hot or cold, moist or dry. So, for example, they believed fire was a pure combination of hot and dry, earth was a pure combination of cold and dry, air was hot and moist, and water was cold and moist.

Alexander, who only lived from 356 BC to 323 BC, became one of the most famous kings in history: Alexander the Great. He conquered most of the world known to the Greeks.

The deep discussions that Aristotle had with the young Alexander were hugely influential. They formed his future ideas about what it meant to be a noble soldier and a good king.

Following the model

Aristotle's followers could use this idea (it would now be called a 'model') to explain what happened when a log was burnt on a fire. First, they said, water oozes out of the ends of the log. Then it produces smoke, which they said was a kind of air. The flames, pretty obviously, are fire, and what you end up with, the ash, is a kind of earth. So they thought a log was made of water, air, fire and earth. Of course, the same explanation wouldn't work if you put a lump of copper or a piece of glass in the fire. But the Greeks ignored anything that didn't fit in with their model.

The fifth element

The word 'quintessence' comes from the medieval Latin word for the number five, quintus. It describes the essence of a thing in its purest and most concentrated form.

What about the heavenly bodies – the Sun, Moon and stars? They couldn't be made of any of the four elements, because they were thought to be perfect and unchanging. So they must be made of something else, a special fifth element, which the Greeks called 'quintessence'.

This idea of perfection, and especially of heavenly perfection, was very important to the Ancient Greeks. Circles are perfect, according to them, because they look the same from all sides, and there is no way to tell one part of the circle from another part. The heavens had to be perfect, because that was where the gods lived; indeed, to them the planets were gods.

In the centre of it all

The Greeks believed that the Earth was at the centre of the Universe, and that the Sun and stars moved in circles round the Earth. They thought the stars were lights attached to a hollow sphere, like a football, with the Earth in the middle.

But this model didn't work very well for the planets. From the surface of the Earth, it looks as if the planets move along complicated, looping tracks, wandering among the stars.

In order to keep with their idea of circles, the Greeks had to imagine that the planets were fixed to layers of spheres, nested one inside the other like the skins of an onion.

Then they had to imagine that these spheres rotated in circles at different angles to one another and at different speeds, in a complicated way. At the time of Aristotle, the Greek model needed fifty-five separate spheres to explain the motion of the planets! Hardly surprisingly, when an astronomer called Ptolemy came along in the second century with a simpler model, the philosophers welcomed it.

The word 'planet' comes from the Greek word planētēs, *which means 'wanderer'.*

Ptolemy and the planets

Very little is known about Ptolemy, who lived in Alexandria, Egypt, from AD 100–AD 170. We do know that he wrote a famous book called *The Mathematical Compilation*, which summed up what people thought about astronomy in those days and described how they thought the planetary system worked. This explanation is called the Ptolemaic system. Each planet is supposed to move in a small circle round a point, which itself moves in a big circle round the Earth. The small circle was called an 'epicycle', and this idea of cycles, epicycles and loops within loops lasted until the end of the sixteenth century – almost 1,500 years.

Arab mathematicians called Ptolemy's book the *Almagest,* meaning 'the Greatest', which shows how highly esteemed it was.

Moving Forward

The Greeks had several ideas that seem strange to us today. One of them was their solution to the puzzle of why things fall down, like an apple falling off a tree. Aristotle had a neat explanation. He said that things made of fire, earth, air or water will always try to get back to their proper place. So bubbles rise up through water, trying to get to the air, and solid things like apples fall to the earth, where they once grew.

Hitting the Spot

One of the strangest things that Aristotle believed was that if you dropped a heavy thing and a light thing at the same time, the heavy thing would fall faster and hit the ground sooner. Perhaps he had been watching things like feathers or leaves fall slowly through the air, and things like apples fall quickly to the ground. He didn't realize that very light things are slowed down by the resistance of the air, like the drag you feel if you push your hand through water. But if he had just held a big pebble in one hand and a small pebble in the other hand and dropped them at the same time, he would have seen them hit the ground together. To us, it seems amazing that Aristotle never did that simple experiment.

Testing ideas by experiment only really began in Queen Elizabeth I's time. If the Ancient Greeks had realized this was the way to go about science, they might have worked out everything we know long ago – perhaps even before the birth of Jesus Christ?

It's also amazing that for hundreds of years afterwards people believed Aristotle must be right and never thought to try it out for themselves.

Falling into place

Even towards the end of the sixteenth century, many people were astonished when a Dutchman named Simon Stevin, actually performed the experiment. He dropped two lead balls – one ten times heavier than the other – out of the upstairs window of a house on to a wooden board, and listened for the sounds they made when they hit it. It was a single thump, showing that the balls hit the ground at the same moment.

In the 1970s, Apollo astronauts dropped a hammer and a feather simultaneously while they were on the Moon (where there is no air to resist their motion). They hit the ground together.

Aristotle and animals

Aristotle did much better with biology. As far as we know, he was the first person who tried to describe all the different kinds of animals that were known, to understand their structure, how they reproduce and how their bodies work.

With animals Aristotle sometimes did the kinds of experiments that he should have done when working out the laws of motion. For instance, the Greeks thought that an elephant could never lie down, because its legs could not bend properly, so they must have to sleep leaning against trees. Aristotle didn't have any live elephants to observe but he studied the leg joints of an elephant skeleton and proved that they would work perfectly well to let the elephant lie down to sleep.

The most interesting animal of all, though – to us at least – is the human animal. Everything the ancients knew about human anatomy was summed up by a Greek physician named Claudius Galenus, usually known simply as Galen.

In his studies of bees, Aristotle made one mistake. He thought that, like Greece, the hive was run by a king, not by a queen. The idea that any kind of society – even insects' – could be ruled by females was unthinkable in those days!

Galen

The first and most influential anatomist, he was doctor to gladiators and emperors, and left behind a wealth of work about the human body.

Galen became a physician to several important Roman emperors, including Marcus Aurelius, who became a friend of his.

Galen lived from about AD 130 to about AD 200 (about 500 years after Aristotle). He was lucky enough to be born in a rich part of the great Roman Empire. Any troubles there might be on the borders of the Empire had little influence on life in the quiet town of Pergamum.

Galen's father was a well-off architect and farmer. With an important place in society, he could easily afford to make sure that his son had the best possible education. When Galen was sixteen his father had a powerful dream in which he saw the figure of Asclepius, the god of medicine and healing. He took this to be an important sign for the future: his son would become a doctor.

Galen and the gladiators

Most gladiators were slaves or war captives, forced to fight for bloodthirsty Roman audiences. Good fighters, who pleased the crowds, could eventually earn their freedom. But many more were killed or terribly wounded.

Galen started his medical studies in his hometown, but when he was nineteen his father died, leaving him plenty of money. He was able to travel and study wherever he wanted, so he spent much of the next nine years studying in cities like Alexandria and Corinth. When he came back to Pergamum as a fully fledged doctor, he got a job as Chief Physician for the gladiators in the city, a very prestigious job. Tending the terrible injuries of the gladiators gave him plenty of first-hand opportunities to become familiar with human anatomy. It was a valuable experience for the young Galen.

Unfortunately for science, though, at that time nobody was allowed to dissect a human, not even the body of a gladiator or a criminal. This made it very difficult for Galen to find out the proper workings of the body. Instead he had to dissect animals, such as apes, dogs and pigs, and try to guess if there were any similarities to humans.

Galen was a particular admirer of Hippocrates, a famous doctor who had lived from about 460 BC to about 370 BC. But he didn't think much of the other doctors he met during his career, and he often criticized them, on one occasion calling them 'snotty-nosed individuals'. He was an exceptionally clever person who did not suffer fools gladly.

Hippocrates believed all illness had a physical explanation. He firmly rejected the old ideas that sickness was caused by things such as evil spirits or falling out of favour with the gods.

Galen's legacy

Galen wrote a great deal about medicine and, fortunately, much of what he wrote survived. He summed up what people at the time thought about medicine, just as Ptolemy summed up what people thought about astronomy.

Galen's book on human anatomy was almost as good as it could have been, given that he was never able to perform proper dissections. The trouble was, as with Aristotle, for centuries afterwards people had such respect for Galen that they didn't question his work – even when they had the opportunity to cut up a body for themselves and find out where he had gone wrong.

So why was it that later generations held the ideas of the Greeks and Romans in such awe – and for more than 1,000 years?

Divide of the mighty Empire

The modern name of the city of Constantinople is Istanbul, now the capital of Turkey.

At its greatest, the Roman Empire stretched from Britain in the west, to Asia Minor (where modern countries like Turkey are located) in the east, including Egypt and most of the northern edge of Africa. It was very difficult to run such a large empire from Rome, especially when the rulers of the Empire were squabbling among themselves over who should run it. By the fourth century AD the Empire had been split into two halves. The western half (mostly the countries now known as Britain, France, Spain and Italy) was ruled from Rome, and the official language was Latin. The eastern half was ruled from a city at first called Byzantium and later Constantinople. The official language of this half of the Empire was Greek, and it became known as the Byzantine Empire.

The dawn of the Dark Ages

The Dark Ages got their name because very few books were written in western Europe during that time – and ever fewer survived – so we know very little about what went on in that period.

The western Empire didn't last long. By AD 476 it had been overrun by barbarians, the city of Rome had fallen, and most of its books were lost or destroyed. This was the beginning of the period (from about AD 500 to about AD 1000) known as the Dark Ages.

During this time there were many wars, and people like the Vikings wreaked havoc before things eventually settled down and Europe started to become civilized once again.

Things were different in the east where the Byzantine Empire survived and flourished. But Byzantium was often at war too, and it didn't make any great advances in scientific knowledge. Its scientific resources lay in its libraries, in which copies of Roman and Greek books were kept.

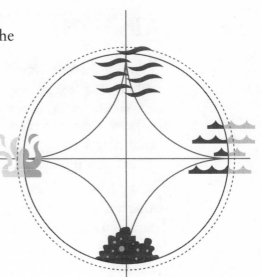

The end of an empire

After the Prophet Mohammed established the religion of Islam in the seventh century, the Islamic civilization dominated the Middle East and spread along North Africa and even into Spain. The Byzantine Empire shrank until eventually the city of Constantinople itself was taken by the Ottoman Turks in 1453 – almost 1,000 years after the fall of Rome. This was the end of the Roman Empire.

Copies of the Greek and Roman books were made and passed on to other people, especially the Arabic scholars who were their neighbours.

Despite the 'Dark Ages' name, things were nowhere near as dark for the history of the Byzantine Empire or the Islamic civilization, because many books were written at that time. So it is more appropriate to call these 1,000 years from AD 500 to AD 1500 the Middle Ages – the middle between the fall of Rome, and the beginning of our modern civilization, in which science is so important.

Alhazen

The greatest scientist of the Middle Ages – and the first to have the confidence to improve on the ideas of the ancient Greeks.

Abu Ali al-Hasan ibn Al-Haitham, usually known simply as Alhazen, lived almost exactly in the middle of the Middle Ages, from about AD 965 to AD 1039. Alhazen was born in the city of Basra, which is now part of Iraq, but he later moved to Cairo, the new capital of Egypt.

A dangerous day job

Aswan now has a huge and very successful dam. It has helped counter the effects of flooding and droughts.

Alhazen was the adviser to Caliph al-Hakim, a mad tyrant who ruled Egypt at the time. Working for a mad tyrant was a dangerous job, and Alhazen made a mistake that nearly cost him his life: he boasted that he knew how to control the flooding of the River Nile. He told the caliph that he could construct a dam that would enable water to be stored for irrigating the fields during times of drought. Alhazen also said that the dam would help to prevent flooding when torrential rains came.

It was only when he arrived at the site of the proposed dam at Aswan that Alhazen realized he had totally underestimated the difficulties. He had to face the fact that he didn't have nearly enough money or men to complete the task. He also knew that if he went back and confessed this to the caliph he would be put to death.

Acting the part

Alhazen's only hope of escape was to pretend to be

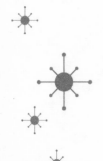

mad – because Islamic law forbade the execution of a lunatic. To avoid death Alhazen had to keep up the pretence of being insane for twelve years, until Caliph al-Hakim died in 1021. All this time Alhazan lay low in Cairo, studying and teaching.

But Alhazen had done all his important scientific work around the end of the tenth century, long before working for the caliph. This work involved the study of light (optics), and it was important for two reasons. Firstly, he got a lot of it right. But secondly, and just as important, he worked out his ideas for himself, did experiments and didn't just accept what the Greeks had said.

Alhazen's life-saving pretence of insanity meant that he was not able to lead a completely normal life again until he was fifty-six years old.

Seeing the light

Alhazen managed to work out the puzzle of eyesight. The Greeks thought that our eyes sent out some kind of influence to probe the world outside, like invisible feelers. But Alhazen realized that light is made inside things that shine, like the Sun or the flame of a candle. The light travels from them to our eyes, and everywhere else, in straight lines. We are able to see things that don't shine because light from the Sun, or something else that shines, bounces off them and into our eyes.

This kind of darkened room is called a 'camera obscura', which means 'darkened chamber' and gives us the modern word 'camera'.

A Frenchman named René Descartes proved Kepler was right. He took the eye from a dead ox and scraped the back wall until it was so thin it became transparent. He was able to see the image made on the retina by the light coming in through the pupil of the eye.

To show how this worked, Alhazen made a tiny hole in the curtain of a darkened room, which let light from outside in. The light made an image of the world outside on the wall opposite the curtains.

Alhazen also studied the way light is bent by lenses and reflected by mirrors, and the nature of rainbows. But after he died in Cairo in 1039, nobody took much notice of his ideas for many years. Then, in 1572, more than 500 years after his death, his book was printed in Latin. Called *Opticae Thesaurus* (*The Treasury of Optics*), it was published at a momentous time.

A scientific awakening

Science was just beginning to take off in Europe, and this time people noticed how much better Alhazen's ideas were than those of the ancients. A German man called Johannes Kepler (who was born the year before *Opticae Thesaurus* was published) used it as a stepping stone to learn even more about optics. It was Kepler who realized that the human eye is almost exactly like a camera obscura. Light goes in through the pupil of the eye in the same way that it goes through the hole in the curtain, and makes an image on the retina at the back of the eye in the same way that it makes an image on the wall at the back of the camera obscura.

But why was it that 500 years after Alhazen died people were suddenly interested in his work, and in all kinds of science? There were many reasons why science took off around that time, but one of the most important was the fall of Constantinople. People began inventing the modern world almost literally out of the ashes of the last remnant of the Roman Empire.

Into the Light

A besieged city causes hundreds of people to flee to Italy. Their arrival sparks off an explosion of exciting new ideas in Europe.

Even in the face of impending doom, the people of Constantinople – there were 50,000 left – defended themselves to the bitter end. But after a bloody two-month siege, the city was overrun and all the inhabitants killed or enslaved.

Long before the Turks conquered Constantinople in 1453, it was clear that the city was doomed. Anyone who had any sense got out before the battle began and many scholars and artists fled to Italy, where their ideas and accomplishments would be valued.

Italy was an exciting place to be in the fifteenth century. The country was split into many city states, each ruled by a prince or duke, and these states were constantly vying with each other, their disagreements sometimes leading to all-out war.

To be the best

This competitive environment was very beneficial to the new immigrants. Every prince wanted to win and have the best of everything. Consequently, the best artists, the best musicians, the best mathematicians and philosophers became trophies to be gathered at court, to show the world that he was more cultured and wealthy than his rivals. Once again, science flourished because society was rich enough to afford scientists.

Italy was transformed by the flood of bright people, books and ideas. It began to buzz with artistic and intellectual activity, lapping up the new knowledge and culture. And by a fortunate coincidence, all of this happened around the same time as a technological advance that would revolutionize the way knowledge was accessed – printing, using moveable type.

This method – in which each letter is set on a

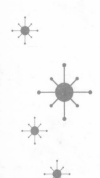

separate cast-metal block and can be moved around at will – had been developed in 1455 in Germany. It was a much more flexible method than any other used previously.

A Print Revolution

Up until now books had been scarce and precious, having been laboriously produced – copied either by hand or by engraving the text on to wooden blocks. Now, for the first time in history, it was possible to produce hundreds of copies of a book with relative ease, making the knowledge they contained accessible to a much wider audience.

Although this wasn't quite communication for all – most of the poor could neither read nor afford to buy books – printing using movable type did mean that suddenly there were many more books about. Just fifty years after its introduction, 500,000 books were in circulation.

Many of these books had originally been brought to the western world by the fleeing Byzantine scholars. As well as texts of Arab learning – Alhazan's famous book on optics was published in 1572, for instance – many of the 'new' books from the Arab world were actually texts from Ancient Greece. These great works had been translated into Latin, then Arabic, and copied by hand in Constantinople. One way or another, a huge amount of knowledge survived from Ancient Greece.

Reinventing the Wheel

The European scholars of the fifteenth

The fifteenth century printing revolution can be compared to the invention of the internet in the twentieth century. Both brought about a new and massive change in the way information was spread.

Before the invention of printing, books were so precious that many were chained in the libraries of religious institutions – there is still a 'chain library' in Hereford Cathedral, England.

century were amazed and impressed by the great learning and discoveries of the ancients. Faced with this mass of knowledge, they at first lost confidence in themselves, believing that they could discover nothing new. Surely, they reasoned, anything that they found out about the way the world works would only be rediscovering things the Greeks must have known already?

we can do better

But, over time, people began to realize that the Greeks had not been right about everything. Discoveries were being made that were actually brand new ideas, ones that the Greeks hadn't known about at all.

Suddenly anything was possible. Scholars could build on ancient knowledge or reject it. All aspects of science, art, music and philosophy were open to new ideas, styles and interpretations. Here was a new beginning for European civilization. This incredibly exciting period of intellectual and cultural activity became known as the Renaissance.

'Renaissance' literally means 'rebirth'; civilization had been born again.

Science lagged a little way behind art and culture at the beginning of the Renaissance. It took time for books to be translated, ideas to spread. By coincidence, two great books on science were published in the same year, 1543, ninety years after the fall of Constantinople. One was about astronomy and the place of the Earth in the Universe; the other was about anatomy and the place of humankind in the animal kingdom. Their appearance can be used to mark the beginning of the scientific Renaissance. And almost exactly 1,000 years after the fall of Rome, the author of the first of these remarkable books was born.

The Renaissance began in 1453, with the fall of Constantinople, and it ended about 250 years later.

Nicolaus copernicus

The man who came up with the biggest astronomical idea the world had ever seen. But would anyone believe him?

In 1473, in the town of Torun, Poland, a baby son was born to a rich merchant. Named Mikolaj Kopernik, his story is a good example of how you had to be rich to be a scientist in those days.

A man of influence

Sadly, Mikolaj's father died when he was only ten years old, so he was sent to live with his uncle, who was a powerful bishop. His uncle used his influence to make sure his nephew was well educated and, among other things, Mikolaj learnt Latin, a very important language in those days. When he came to write his own books, Mikolaj used a Latin version of his name – Nicolaus Copernicus – the name by which we still know him today.

When he was eighteen, Nicolaus was sent to university in Krakow, Poland. He had a brilliant, restless mind and did extremely well there. Five years later he moved to Italy, the powerhouse of the Renaissance, and there he studied law and medicine. But his interest was sparked off by a completely different subject when he rented rooms from a

Latin was used for centuries after the fall of the Roman Empire because it was the official language of the Christian church. Important books were printed in Latin and all educated Europeans learnt it.

Copernicus's uncle had found him a sinecure – a job where he got paid but could get away with doing nothing.

Copernicus also worked as a doctor and legal adviser at this time. He helped look after the sick among the poor people of Frombork.

professor of astronomy. Nicolaus became fascinated by the subject too, spending his spare time helping with the professor's observations. For the time being, however, astronomy would have to remain a hobby for the young student.

Jobs for the boys

After qualifying as a medical doctor, Nicolaus studied for yet another degree in church law. A perpetual student, whose money gave him the time to do nothing but learn, he also fell on his feet when, thanks again to his uncle, he was appointed as a canon at Frombork Cathedral, back home in Poland. The job should really have involved looking after both the cathedral and the worshippers, but, in fact, other people were doing that work already.

Copernicus didn't even bother to live at Frombork. Instead he stayed in Italy for another three years, studying the classical literature of Greece and Rome that had come to Italy with the fall of Constantinople. More importantly, he was able to indulge in his great hobby, astronomy.

But he couldn't carry on being a student forever and in 1506 Copernicus returned to Poland to work for his uncle until the old man died in 1512. It was during this time that Copernicus developed his revolutionary astronomical idea – that the *Earth* moves round the Sun.

A Shocking idea

This was an incredible new concept. Up until then everyone believed that the Earth was the centre of the Universe.

Copernicus first described this idea in a short manuscript called *Commentariolus* (Latin for '*Little Commentary*') and showed it to his friends around 1510. But he didn't publish it because some details still worried him. However, several copies of the manuscript were made and one went to Rome, where the Pope and several important churchmen attended a lecture on his work.

Interruptions

Astronomy then had to take a back seat for two years, as after his uncle's death Copernicus had to take his duties as Canon a lot more seriously. When he was finally able to devote himself to his astronomy again, he bought a house and had a special platform built for viewing the skies with all his astronomical instruments.

War breaks out

More interruptions occurred in 1519 in the form of war between Poland and the German Teutonic Knights. Copernicus showed an unexpected talent as a man of action when the region was attacked by their army in 1520.

With work and wars to contend with, life had become increasingly busy for Copernicus and he never found the time to write down all of his ideas. He was nearly seventy years old when one day he received a visitor from Germany who had heard about his incredible idea of the Earth revolving

The Greek astronomer Aristarchus of Samos had also suggested that the Earth moves round the Sun, in the third century BC. But most of his fellow Greeks thought this was a crazy idea. Copernicus knew nothing about Aristarchus – he came up with the idea by himself.

Copernicus was in charge of the defences at Allenstein Castle. Under his leadership the castle held out against the invading army for several months until the invasion was repelled.

Ptolemy's work, the Almagest, *was brought to Europe by the scholars fleeing Constantinople and had been used as the model for the Universe ever since.*

round the Sun.

This visitor was Georg Joachim von Lauchen, known as Rheticus. He was a professor of mathematics in Germany, an important position, but when he heard about Copernicus's idea he became so excited that he gave up his job and travelled to Frombork to meet the great man himself.

The thinking behind it all

How had Copernicus come up with this idea? Why did he question Ptolemy's model of the Universe, in which all the planets were shown to revolve round the Earth?

The only other person who had questioned Ptolemy was a German scientist called Regiomontanus, who died in 1476. He identified several problems with Ptolemy's idea in his book, the *Epitome*. The worst problem was that, in order for Ptolemy's theory to work, the Moon had to be much closer to the Earth at some times than others. If this were the case then the Moon should look a lot bigger at the times it was closest to Earth. But of course it doesn't.

The Epitome *was published in 1496, the year twenty-three-year-old Copernicus went to Italy to study. It was one of the first books he read there, and it set him thinking.*

The Sun is the centre

Copernicus's solution to these problems was to make the Sun, not the Earth, the centre of the Universe. Using this model, the planets could move in orbits centred on the Sun and the Moon could always orbit the Earth at more or less the same distance, so it would always look about the same size. This wasn't just a wild guess. Copernicus worked out the whole theory with great care using geometry. He then imagined an invisible sphere surrounding the Sun, Moon and planets, on which the stars were fixed. Instead of the whole of this sphere rotating round the

Earth once every twenty-four hours (as suggested by Ptolemy) Copernicus said that the way the stars and Sun appear to move across the sky could be explained if the Earth turned on its axis once every twenty-four hours.

close to the truth

Copernicus's ideas completely changed what people thought about the Universe, and in many respects he was right. The Earth and planets *do* orbit the Sun, but the Sun is not the centre of the Universe, just our own Solar System. He was also right that the Earth turns on its axis approximately once every twenty-four hours, but we now know that the stars aren't little lights fixed to the inside of a distant sphere, but are huge fiery objects like the Sun, scattered at different distances across space.

To us, having grown up knowing that the Sun is at the centre of the Solar System, it all seems so obvious that it's hard to understand just how difficult it was for people living 500 years ago to believe.

science versus common sense

The problem was that although the geometry worked, nothing about the idea made sense to people. If the Earth was whizzing round the Sun, why didn't people feel a constant rush of air speeding past them, the way they would when they were riding a galloping horse? And if it were spinning on its axis, how come if you dropped a cannonball from the top of a tall tower it fell at the bottom of the tower, and didn't get left behind as the Earth moved round?

Today, we explain this in terms of 'inertia' –

The Moon takes just over twenty-seven days to orbit the Earth, and also turns once on its axis at the same time. So it always shows the same side facing the Earth. Nobody had seen the far side of the Moon until spaceships went there in the 1960s.

Copernicus knew nothing about inertia, and these puzzles made him have doubts about his idea. That's probably why he didn't publish his ideas back in 1510.

things keep moving the way they are already moving unless something happens to stop them. So the air keeps moving along with the Earth, and the falling cannonball isn't just falling down, it's also rotating along with the Earth, because there's nothing to stop it.

> The truth about inertia was very neatly demonstrated by Frenchman Pierre Gassendi in 1640, nearly 100 years after Copernicus died. Gassendi borrowed a galley – a ship rowed by banks of oarsmen – from the French navy. The galley was the fastest, smoothest way to travel in those days (at least until the rowers got tired) and he got the oarsmen to row it flat out across the still waters of the Mediterranean. While it was moving at top speed, his assistant dropped heavy balls from the top of the mast. Instead of being left behind by the ship's motion, the balls fell at the bottom of the mast. Because of inertia, they kept moving forward at the same speed as the galley all the time they were falling.

Publish and be damned

After he had spoken to Copernicus about his theories Rheticus wrote a short account of the model, which was published in 1540 with the grand title *Narratio Prima de Libris Revolutionum Copernici* (*The First Account of the Revolutionary Book by Copernicus*). He persuaded Copernicus to finish his own book,

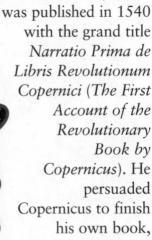

and took the manuscript back to Germany with him so that he could have it printed.

Rheticus never saw Copernicus again. In 1542 he moved to a new job and city, leaving the printing of *De Revolutionibus Orbium Coelestium* (*On the Revolution of the Celestial Spheres*) to be overseen by Andreas Osiander, a priest.

Osiander was a follower of Martin Luther, a fervent religious reformer who lived from 1483 to 1546. Luther strongly objected to the Copernican model, largely because there is a passage in the Bible where the Sun is commanded to stand still. If the Sun wasn't moving across the sky, how could it be commanded to stop moving?

Luther was the leader of a movement known as the Reformation, which attacked the corruption in the Roman Catholic Church and wanted to get back to the basic religion taught in the Bible. His followers were known as Protestants.

Cautiously, Osiander added a preface to the book – without telling Copernicus – saying that the model wasn't supposed to describe how the Universe really is. He said it was all a kind of mathematical trick you could use to make it easier to calculate the orbits of the planets. His meddling didn't work – Copernicus's idea was condemned by Luther's followers anyway.

Copernicus's great work was finally published in 1543. It's surprising, but nobody took much notice of the book, at first. Copernicus died the same year and although there is a touching story that he saw a copy of the book while he was on his deathbed, this is probably just a legend; most likely, he never saw his book at all. Rheticus kept proclaiming the book's greatness, but he died in 1576 having failed to convince the world. That year, the person who would finally make people sit up and take notice of the Copernican model, Galileo Galilei, was just twelve years old. But before we come to his story, we must return to the other great book published in 1543, and the man who wrote it.

Andreas Vesalius

The first person to properly dissect the human body, this great anatomist was at one time forced to steal the dead bodies of criminals for his research.

Vesalius was Flemish, from a country called Flanders (which no longer exists). It used to encompass parts of what are now Belgium, the Netherlands and France.

Andreas Vesalius was born in Brussels in 1514. Like Copernicus, Vesalius never had to worry about where the next penny was coming from. He came from a long line of physicians in royal service; his father was Court Pharmacist to Charles V and his grandfather was also Charles' physician.

Vesalius decided to study medicine too, upholding his family tradition. But his studies at the University of Louvain, Belgium, were soon rudely interrupted.

Turbulent times

Charles V was often at war with the French and other neighbours, and he tried unsuccessfully to crush Martin Luther's Protestant movement. Vesalius got caught up in this turmoil. In 1533 he went to Paris – one of the best places to study medicine at the time – to become a doctor. It was here that Vesalius first became fascinated by anatomy, retrieving bones from graveyards and execution sites for examination. His first proper dissections were on animals and he became so knowledgeable that he was asked to give a public lecture to his fellow students and teachers. But when war broke out in 1536, he was forced to return to Louvain.

Apparently Vesalius kept body parts in his room for several days, until the smell became unbearable.

Dedicated to dissection

The facilities in Louvain were so bad that the only way Vesalius could carry on his study of human anatomy was to go out at dead of night to steal the body of a criminal. He would have to get the hanging body down from the gibbet outside the city, and take it back to his room to dissect.

With such enthusiasm, and his training in Paris, Vesalius had no trouble qualifying as a doctor in 1537. With the war still raging, he moved on to the University of Padua in Italy. Here Vesalius found it much easier to get hold of fresh bodies. The university had an arrangement with the local authorities for bodies of executed criminals to be handed over for dissection.

As there was no way of refrigerating bodies at that time, this was an important step forward for Vesalius and was a far cry from his student days when he had to keep bits of rotting body under the bed . . .

There was one judge who would let Vesalius choose the time of execution, so that the criminal's body would be fresh when he needed it for a lecture.

Anatomical errors

Proper dissection was incredibly important to Vesalius. His predecessor, Galen, had never been able to dissect real bodies and this would have held him back hugely. But when the professors in the Italian universities started to teach anatomy, based on Galen's book, they were able to cut open real corpses. But they didn't make the most of this opportunity. Why should they when Galen's book contained everything they needed to know?

When a professor was teaching anatomy, he would sit on a platform, or stand at a lectern, with

As with the other Greeks, people at first thought of Galen as some kind of Greek superhero who had found out everything there was to know about the human body.

In those days, the surgeon was regarded as a low-class, manual worker who was just good at cutting things up. Many surgeons doubled up as barbers when they weren't cutting up corpses.

Galen's book open in front of him, and read out the relevant part. Meanwhile another man – the surgeon – would cut up the body on the table in front of the students, to expose the organs the professor was talking about.

During the dissection a third man – the ostensor – would use a long pointer to show the students which bits of the body the professor was referring to. It was difficult for the students to see anything and the professor generally paid little attention to the dissection itself. All in all it was a very unsatisfactory way of learning about the intricacies of the human body.

Getting it right

One of the artists was John Stephen of Kalkar, who was a pupil of the great artist Titian.

Unlike these teachers, Vesalius performed his own dissections and clearly explained what he was uncovering to his students as he went along.

He soon found out where Galen had gone wrong, and he paid excellent artists to make drawings of the things he dissected. The drawings were not only perfectly accurate, but beautiful works of art as well.

Vesalius summed up his discoveries in his illustrated book *De Humani Corporis Fabrica* (*On the Structure of the Human Body*), published in 1543, the same year that Copernicus published his great book.

Despite his wonderfully detailed work, traditionalists in Italy still thought that Galen was perfect, and criticized Vesalius for trying to improve upon it. It was probably because of this that he gave up teaching and used his connections to get a job as Court Physician to Emperor Charles V. The emperor was forced to abdicate in 1555, but not before he had given Vesalius, who was only forty-two, a title and a pension for life.

There was a plentiful supply of bodies for Vesalius, as the death penalty applied for many crimes in those days.

The wrong job

Despite his pension Vesalius preferred to continue working and promptly got the job of Physician at the court of Philip II in Spain. But this was a big mistake. Spain was very backward compared with Italy. The doctors there still followed Galen to the letter and resented Vesalius and his new ideas. The fact that Vesalius came from the Netherlands – then a Spanish territory that was fighting for its independence from Spain – also counted against him. It seemed there was no way out for Vesalius – the job was for life; Vesalius wasn't *allowed* to resign, or even to leave Spain without the king's permission. He had to find a way out.

A disastrous end

In 1564 Vesalius asked Philip for permission to go on a pilgrimage to Jerusalem. The king agreed. He had no idea that Vesalius had plans to 'stop off' in Italy on the return journey! But Vesalius's escape plan never came off. His ship ran into severe storms and, with supplies running low, and the passengers half-starved and desperately seasick, it ran aground on the Greek island of Zakinthos in October 1564. There, Vesalius became ill and died. But he had already provided the inspiration for a younger generation of anatomists, who were finding out more and more about how the human body works.

Vesalius's followers

The Fallopian tubes are internal organs that carry eggs from the ovaries into the uterus.

The first of these was Gabriello Fallopio – known as Fallopius – one of Vesalius's students in Padua. He went on to become Professor of Anatomy in Pisa in 1548, and later came back to Padua to take up Vesalius's old job. He made his own investigations of the human body and, among other things, he discovered the organs still known as the Fallopian tubes.

But the most important thing he did was to pass on Vesalius's ideas to his own students – including the principle that you should do your own dissections to find out how the body works, and not rely on books.

Fallopius died in 1562, two years before Vesalius. But he was succeeded by his student Girolamo Fabrizio, born in 1537 in the town of Aquapendente. He later changed his name to the more impressive Hieronymous Fabricius ab Aquapendente.

Fabricius taught Vesalius's ideas to hundreds of students during his long career, and also did some important work himself. He had a special lecture theatre built in Padua, designed so that all the students could see what was going on at dissections – a far cry from the days of old.

One discovery he made (that he showed to his students) were the tiny valves inside the veins. Fabricius never quite realized their significance.

The man who did that was an English physician – William Harvey – who attended Fabricius's lectures. His story, and the story of another English doctor – William Gilbert – show how much science had moved on between 1543 and the 1600s.

The valves that Fabricius discovered stop blood in the veins flowing away from the heart.

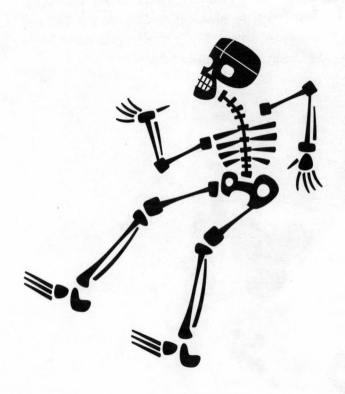

Three Men and...

a Buzzing fly

Three Men and a Buzzing Fly

Nowadays, we know so much about science that if you study it at university you will have to concentrate on just one area – for example, physics, biology or chemistry.

If you wanted to study science in the 1500s and 1600s, it helped if you were wealthy, well educated and well connected. All these were certainly true of the three scientists in this chapter. Between them they made some amazing discoveries about three very different phenomena – magnetism, electricity and the circulation of the blood.

How much do you know about science? In Queen Elizabeth I's time, if you were clever enough, you could have learnt just about all there *was* to know. Because there was so much still to be discovered, you would also have had a great opportunity to find out something new.

Learning and earning

In Elizabethan times, you'd have to pay for all your board and lodgings at university and there were no grants or student loans to help you.

If you wanted to study science in Elizabethan England, one of the best ways to go about it was to become a doctor. But before you could be a doctor, you needed something else first – money. University courses were expensive, and you had to spend years studying to get your degree.

But if you could scrape the money together – or persuade a rich relative or acquaintance to help you out – you could earn a lot once you qualified. As a doctor, you would also have plenty of spare time to study other subjects that interested you.

Another advantage of studying medicine, although it might not sound like it, was that you would learn Latin and Greek. Most books, including medical textbooks, were written in these ancient languages, so you needed to be fluent. All in all, it's not surprising that lots of early scientists were also doctors (called 'physicians' in those days).

william Gilbert

one of the doctors at queen Elizabeth's court would one day be thought of as England's first real scientist. His name was william Gilbert.

Luckily for Gilbert, who was born in Colchester, Essex, in 1544, his father was an important man, the recorder of Colchester (a kind of junior judge), who could easily afford that essential expensive education for his son. In 1558, the year Elizabeth was crowned, William went to Cambridge University at just fourteen years old. Although this sounds extraordinarily young to become a student, it was actually quite common in those days.

Undergraduates were really only expected to study the Greek and Roman classics. Just a few, like Gilbert, went on to more advanced things. He chose to pursue medicine and he finally qualified as a doctor when he was twenty-five. He was then offered a job at St John's College in Cambridge, which gave him enough money to enjoy a very comfortable lifestyle: he had a place to live, servants, friends and time to devote to his own studies.

Only one in ten people reached the age of forty in Tudor times, so it is not so surprising that people studied, married and had children when they were still very young.

The first real scientist

Gilbert was fascinated by magnetism, and for the next four years he spent much of his time experimenting with magnets and electricity. It is these experiments that set Gilbert apart and make him worthy of being regarded as the first proper scientist.

Experiments require a logical approach. First of all you need a theory or idea. Then you devise an experiment to test that idea. You do the experiment, note down the results and draw a conclusion from what you have seen happen, just the same as you still do in science lessons today. Here are a couple of Gilbert's experiments:

The nature of attraction . . .

The Ancient Greeks had noticed that when amber (fossilized tree resin) is rubbed, it attracts tiny objects, such as little pieces of paper or straw, to itself.

The Greeks thought that the amber attracted things because it was warm. Gilbert decided to test this idea. He warmed up a piece of amber – without rubbing it – to see if it still attracted things; it didn't. From this he was able to say that it wasn't the heat that attracted the tiny pieces of paper and straw, but another, invisible force. Today we call that force 'static electricity'; the same thing that makes your hair crackle if you pull a nylon shirt over your head on a still, dry day.

. . . and the art of repulsion

Gilbert loved to disprove superstitious ideas by logically testing them out. In another experiment, for instance, he tested an old wives' tale that a magnet would lose its magnetic power if somebody with repulsive garlicky breath breathed on it. People had believed this for hundreds of years, but hadn't bothered to test it. Gilbert rubbed magnets all over with garlic and – surprise, surprise – found they were still just as magnetic as before.

These experiments seem so simple, and so obvious to us, that it is hard to see why Gilbert's work was so important. But before him, *nobody* had realized that the way to do science properly is to test every idea by experiment and only keep the ideas that pass the tests. 'Strong reasons are obtained from sure experiments,' Gilbert said in his book on magnetism, published in 1600 – and he was right.

Gilbert's book, De Magnete, was very popular – one of the Big Reads of his day – and it was sold all over Europe. Even the great Galileo read it.

A giant magnet

But Gilbert went a lot further than disproving old myths. In one of his most important works, he made some ball magnets and measured the magnetism all round them using tiny magnetic needles. He found that the way the little needles pointed in different directions at different places round these magnetic spheres was just the same as the way a compass needle points in different directions at different places round the Earth. He worked out from this that the Earth itself acts like a giant bar magnet. He even invented the terms North and South Poles, for the opposing ends of bar magnets.

People used to think that compass needles in Britain pointed north because there was a huge island of magnetic rock somewhere off the coast of Scotland.

To infinity, and beyond

Gilbert also had some big ideas about the Universe. He was fascinated by the new idea that the Earth rotated once every day on its axis. However, he thought it was crazy to imagine that the stars could be stuck to the inside of some invisible sphere whirling round the Earth once every twenty-four hours. He realized that the further away from us the stars are, the faster they would have to move to complete the circuit. If they were attached to something, he reasoned, any such structure would surely be 'wrecked and shattered to pieces by such mad and immeasurable velocity (speed)'.

This was another big step forward. Before Gilbert, people thought that the rules that apply on Earth – the rules of physics – didn't apply in the Universe. But Gilbert took it for granted that the same laws of physics applied both to the stars as well as to Earth. These ideas would pave the way for the great thinkers that would come after Gilbert, such as Isaac Newton.

Medic of monarchs

The Royal College of Physicians is the oldest medical society in Britain. It was founded by King Henry VIII in 1518 to improve standards of medical practice.

For all his original scientific thinking, Gilbert wasn't a professional scientist (no such thing existed in those days) and eventually he had to turn his mind to earning a living. He went to London around 1573 and started a very successful career as a doctor. He published his book on magnetism and became an important member of the College of Physicians.

In 1601, Gilbert was given one of the top jobs in his profession, being made one of the physicians in the court of Queen Elizabeth – he was even among the doctors who treated her during her last illness. When Elizabeth died he then worked in the court of her successor, King James I. But, sadly, he didn't serve his new king for long, dying himself, probably of plague, later that year.

About the time Gilbert died, another English doctor – who would also become physician to a king and a famous scientist – had just returned from Padua in Italy, where he had been studying medicine. His name was William Harvey.

William Harvey

A renowned doctor and the first person to discover how our life force works – the pumping heart and the circulation of the blood.

Although Harvey was one of eleven children, his landowner father was still wealthy enough to give his sons a good education. William was the eldest child. He was born in Folkestone in 1578, and was sent off to school in nearby Canterbury when he was just ten years old – in 1588, the year of the Spanish Armada.

William was a good scholar and he decided to study to be a doctor at the best place in England for medicine at the time, Gonville and Caius College, Cambridge. One of the reasons the college was so good was because it had a special charter from the queen that allowed it to have the bodies of two executed criminals each year for dissection. This gave Harvey and his fellow students a head start when it came to anatomy.

Harvey got his degree and then went to Padua where he saw the great anatomist Vesalius in action, dissecting human bodies and pointing out the presence of one-way valves in the veins. This experience would be an important influence on William in his later work.

A glittering career

But that was still in the future. Harvey came back to England and embarked on a hugely successful career. He became a member of the College of Physicians, got married and, in 1618, became Court Physician and a personal friend to

King James I. He went on to serve King Charles I, as well. With a princely income of £400 a year plus free accommodation in the king's palace, Harvey could count his career as an unqualified success.

The man with a hole in his chest

In 1640, Harvey was sent by the king to investigate an apparent miracle. An Irish nobleman Hugh Montgomery had arrived in London and immediately caused a stir throughout the city. For Montgomery, a seemingly healthy young man, had a gaping hole in his chest through which it was possible to see the inside of his body. Harvey found Montgomery 'a sprightly youth with a good complexion'. It was not until Montgomery removed the metal plate that he kept for protection over his chest that Harvey saw the amazing truth. He had a hole in his chest so big that Harvey could put most of his hand into it, and yet this caused no pain. Inside the hole, Harvey was able to feel Hugh Montgomery's heart beating under a layer of skin.

The injury was the result of a childhood accident, which had broken several of Montgomery's ribs. The wound had become infected and had then healed and skinned over. Montgomery's condition gave Harvey a unique opportunity to feel the human heart beating; something that no amount of dissections of dead bodies could ever do.

The heart of the matter

While he was working as a royal physician, Harvey did his most important scientific work – on the motion of the heart and the circulation of the blood.

Ever since the time of Galen, people had thought that there were two kinds of blood in the body. This is probably because they had seen blood that was of two different shades: bright red and dark red. They also believed that blood was made in the liver, and was then 'used up' in the muscles and other organs. They were wrong, of course.

Through his detailed dissections and experiments, Harvey found out that there is only one type of blood, which is constantly travelling round the body in a great loop; it isn't 'used up', but constantly recirculated.

Although Harvey couldn't see them, he deduced that there must be tiny, thread-like connections through which arteries linked up with veins to enable blood to flow back to the heart to start the whole process again.

We now know that arteries carry bright red oxygenated blood away from the heart and lungs to the rest of the body where the oxygen is used up. Veins carry this darker deoxygenated blood back to the heart and lungs.

Experimental proof

The key to the whole thing, Harvey said, went back to the time when he saw Vesalius describing the one-way valves in the veins. The valves only let blood flow one way – towards the heart. They don't let blood flow outwards from the liver in all directions.

Harvey carried out many experiments to test how efficient these valves are. In some experiments he used veins from dead animals, but at other times he experimented on himself. He realized that all the blood from the veins going into the heart had to get out again, or the heart would swell up and burst. He figured that the heart must work like a pump, pushing blood out through the arteries. Arteries don't need valves, because the blood in them is pushed along so strongly by the heart.

Harvey also proved that the idea of the blood being constantly created in the liver was a very impractical one. It was a very simple experiment. He counted the number of heartbeats every minute. He worked out that every half-hour the heart pumped

Harvey tied tight cords round his arm, to stop the flow of blood in the veins, and saw how blood could still escape away towards the heart above the cord, but got piled up in a bulging vein below the cord as it was pushed from behind.

out at least sixteen kilograms of blood. If your body was making, and using up, all that fresh blood, you would have to eat at least sixteen kilograms of food just to make the new blood, *every* half an hour. That's the equivalent of eating twenty large loaves of bread, or a hundred bars of chocolate!

The Coming of the Civil War

During one battle, the king asked Harvey to look after his two young sons. The doctor sat down with them under a hedge and quietly read a book to them . . . until a cannonball landed nearby! They decided to move a little further away from the action.

In 1628, Harvey published his ideas in his book *Du Motu Cordis*, but his views were very controversial and lost him quite a few patients. Then his comfortable life as the king's personal physician was rudely interrupted in the 1640s. The king had been getting increasingly unpopular with Parliament, and eventually violent hostilities between the king's supporters and Parliament broke out on 22 August 1642. The English civil war had begun. The king fled from London and Harvey went with him. Sadly, the Parliamentary army ransacked the king's palace at Whitehall, and Harvey's papers, including his scientific notes, were destroyed.

The king moved to Oxford, and Harvey became the warden of Merton College there. As the civil war rumbled on, Harvey continued his medical research and, in 1651, published a groundbreaking work called *Essays on the Generation of Animals*, which looked at how animals develop from conception to birth.

King Charles I was eventually executed for treason on 30 January 1649.

Harvey survived the political turmoil of the civil war and died in London in 1657 at the age of seventy-nine, content in the knowledge that his medical and scientific genius were recognized throughout Europe. But even Harvey wasn't quite as 'scientific' as his successors. He had always believed that there was some kind of mysterious life force that kept the body going, and that the heart was the source of this force. It was another scientist whose work would change this way of thinking.

René Descartes

The first person to truly recognize that the heart is a mechanical pump was a French philosopher and mathematician who had a fondness for sleeping in ovens.

A Sickly Child

René Descartes was another rich intellectual who didn't have to worry about working for a living. But his early life was touched by tragedy. He was born in La Haye (now called La Haye-Descartes), Brittany, in 1596, the son of a wealthy lawyer. But his mother died when René was still a child and his own health was so poor that his doting father feared that René himself would not live long. But against the odds, René did survive, and the inheritance his mother left him meant that he would never have to worry about money.

When René was eight, his father sent him away to study at a college run by Jesuit (Roman Catholic) priests. The Jesuits were notoriously strict, but René was still so sickly that they let him stay in bed late in the mornings, a habit that stayed with him for the rest of his life. He was academically very bright, particularly at maths, and became a top pupil without having to work overly hard. All this indulgence gave Descartes a taste for soft living that would ultimately prove his downfall.

It was very common in those days for wealthy families to send their sons away to school.

Joining Up

Descartes went on to study law, but in 1618 he did something that seemed completely out of character

for a young man who enjoyed easy living. He suddenly decided to take off to the Netherlands and join the army of the Dutch Prince of Orange. This was not quite as harsh and dangerous as it sounds. He had no intention of becoming a fighting soldier. His idea was to be a military engineer, using his mathematical skills to advise the soldiers on how to build bridges and fortifications.

His real reason for joining the army, though, was to travel and see the world, and he enjoyed the life so much that after his stint with the Prince of Orange he also served in the army of Maximilian, Duke of Bavaria. It was while he was with the duke that one of his greatest mathematical ideas suddenly came to him.

Fly on the wall

Descartes' own account describes himself as 'lazing in an oven' when his inspiration hit him. He probably meant a room warmed by an oven or stove.

It was November 1619 and the duke's army was wintering on the bank of the river Danube. There was nothing much to do and Descartes was lazing in bed watching a fly buzzing around and zigzagging its way across the room.

With a flash of insight, he realized that you could tell exactly where the fly was at any moment by measuring its distance from each of the two walls and the floor of the room where it met in a corner.

Just three numbers would exactly pinpoint the location of the fly.

At a stroke, he had invented the now familiar idea of graphs. The position of a point on a graph drawn on paper is measured by how far it is up the graph (the *y* axis) and how far it is along the graph (the *x* axis). For three dimensions, you just need another axis sticking up out of the paper (the *z* axis).

XYZ

This idea of describing the positions of points on a line drawn on a piece of paper, or points in space, is called the Cartesian system, after Descartes. We use this principle in all sorts of ways without even realizing it. For instance, if you give somebody directions in a city by telling them to go a certain distance north, then a certain distance west to get to the building they are looking for, you are using Cartesian coordinates. And if you also tell them that the office they want is on the third floor of the

With the invention of coordinates, Descartes gave people like Isaac Newton some of the tools they needed to work out their important theories, such as the theory of gravity.

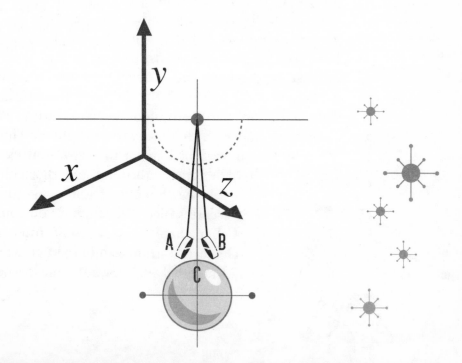

building, you are using three-dimensional Cartesian coordinates.

Descartes' idea transformed science. It meant that scientists could describe any line (for example, the orbit of a planet round the Sun) in terms of numbers and using equations involving x, y and z.

In 1620, Descartes gave up army life and spent nearly ten years travelling about Europe, finally settling in Holland (where he stayed for twenty years), becoming famous as a philosopher and writing up his mathematical ideas in his book called *The Method*.

Ultimately, René was an excellent mathematician, but not a great scientist. Although he came up with plenty of ideas, just like the Ancient Greeks, he didn't bother to test them out.

The life Pump

The heart acts as a simple pump. One side pumps oxygenated blood round the body, the other directs deoxygenated blood to the lungs.

His idea about the heart was one of these. Unlike Harvey, Descartes didn't see any need for a mystical life force to keep the heart pumping. He came up with a mechanical explanation for how the heart worked. He imagined that when blood entered the heart, which was hot, it frothed up and expanded because of the heat. He thought that this pressure would push the valves at the entrance to the heart shut, and stop any more blood getting in until the first lot had escaped into the arteries. His idea sounds more like a steam engine or a modern petrol engine, although neither idea would be thought of until long after Descartes died.

But there is a grain of truth in Descartes' strange and untested ideas. Although Descartes believed in God

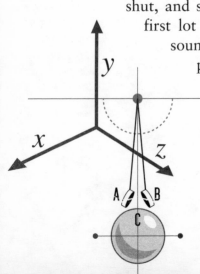

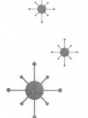

and the soul, he also thought that the human body worked like a machine, and that the soul was something extra. Animals, he thought, had no soul, which proved that you didn't need a soul – or life force – to be alive. This was a daring idea in the 1630s, and a step towards modern thinking – but more of a philosophical step than a scientific one.

Fame and fortune

Descartes became incredibly famous as a philosopher and in 1649 he was invited to Stockholm by Queen Christina of Sweden. She wanted him to teach her philosophy. Comfort-loving Descartes was delighted to be offered what he expected would be a cushy and easy job in the Swedish Court. He didn't bargain for the enthusiasm of the unconventional queen. She wanted her lessons at 5 a.m. every day!

    Poor René hated getting up so early, especially in the dark and cold of the Swedish winter. But there was no way he could resign from such a royal appointment. He did his best, but the combination of early rising and the cold Swedish winter was too much for him. He soon caught a chill, which turned into pneumonia, and he died on 11 February 1650, aged fifty-three.

    The death of Descartes, neatly in the middle of the seventeenth century, is a good place to stop thinking about living things for a while, and go back in time to catch up with how ideas about the Universe changed in the first half of that century. The place to start is just a little bit to the south of Stockholm, in the town of Knudstrup, which was then part of Denmark. And the time to start is December 1546, with the birth of a baby boy christened Tyge.

Christina had become Queen of Sweden at the age of just five. She was a very intelligent person, who had had a strange upbringing. Disappointed that she wasn't born a boy, her father insisted she be brought up as a prince. As an adult she often wore men's clothes.

chapter four

To Infinity and Beyond

To Infinity and Beyond

Europe in the sixteenth and early seventeenth centuries was not always a good place for science. People could be cruelly persecuted for holding views that went against strict religious teachings. However, this didn't hold back three original thinkers when it came to the matter of the universe.

Tycho Brahe

Before he was even two years old, the influential Danish astronomer Tycho Brahe had lost his twin brother, been kidnapped by his uncle and taken away to live in a castle.

Tycho's parents, Otto and Beate, were both from rich and important noble families in Denmark. Otto's brother, Joergen, was also a wealthy man, but sadly he and his wife couldn't have children. In those days it was important for rich families to have a male heir to inherit the family fortune, so Otto had agreed that if he had a son, he would be given to his uncle Joergen to bring up as his heir. But when Tycho and his twin brother were born – in 1546 – Otto and Beate changed their minds. Tycho's twin had died soon after birth, and they didn't want to give away their only surviving son.

Kidnap!

There didn't seem to be anything Joergen could do.

But about a year later Beate had another baby – a boy – and Joergen took matters into his own hands. He kidnapped Tycho. For the next six years Tycho lived with his uncle and aunt in the rather grand surroundings of Tostrup Castle.

A good education

Despite the traumatic events, Tycho's family managed to work things out and the boy stayed at the castle. In fact, Tycho almost certainly benefited from living with his uncle and aunt. Neither of his parents were very interested in education, but Tycho's aunt was keen for him to have a good schooling, so she sent him to a cathedral school at the age of six. Here he studied Latin, something his real father would have considered a waste of time.

When Tycho was twelve, his uncle and aunt sent him to university in the Danish capital city, Copenhagen. The idea was for Tycho to study law so that he could one day go into service for the king. But in 1600 an event occurred that would change the direction of his life.

A shadow on the Sun

In 1600, there was a partial eclipse of the Sun that was visible in Copenhagen. What astounded thirteen-year-old Tycho wasn't so much the eclipse, but the fact that it had been predicted long before.

These predictions were based on observations made of the heavens, going back hundreds of years. Tycho was fascinated, and for the rest of his time in Copenhagen he focused his energies on astronomy and mathematics. Unfortunately, his uncle had other plans and, when Tycho was fifteen, he was sent to another university, in Leipzig, Germany, again, to

Tycho is actually a Latin form of Brahe's original Christian name, Tyge. Scholars often used Latin versions of their names, as it was such an important language.

An eclipse of the Sun happens when the Earth, Moon and Sun line up and the Moon's shadow falls across the Earth, temporarily blocking out the Sun. When only part of the Sun's disc is hidden, it's a partial eclipse.

Measuring the positions with a stick was a tedious job. It was difficult to hold the stick steady, it made your arm ache and it had to be done at night, in the cold! Not many observations were made before Tycho came along.

study law. To make sure he was doing what he was told, his uncle sent along a chaperone, Anders Vedel. But it wasn't much use. Although Tycho studied law well enough to get by, he spent all his money on astronomical instruments and books, and all his spare time reading up about astronomy. When Vedel was asleep, Tycho would creep out of the room they shared to study the stars.

measure for measure

Tycho soon realized that the tables predicting the movements of the Moon and planets that had so fascinated him weren't terribly accurate. They were fine for predicting eclipses, but for other observations the tables could be as much as a month out.

In a way this isn't surprising. Before the telescope was invented, the positions of the stars and planets could only be measured in very crude ways. One method was to hold a stick with a crossbar on it out in front of your eye, and measure how far apart two stars, or a star and a planet, are along the crossbar.

By the time he was sixteen, Tycho realized that the only way to really understand the way the planets move was to keep making these tedious observations as accurately as possible, night after night for years. He decided that this would be his life's work, whatever his uncle might say. But then, in 1563, war broke out between Sweden and Denmark, and his uncle ordered him to come home.

Despite his scientific background, like many people at the time, Tycho believed in astrology. He became an expert at casting horoscopes.

fate steps in

It looked as if Tycho's dream of becoming an astronomer was over. How could he defy his uncle's wishes? Tycho couldn't see a way out – but then his

life took another turn.

The king had been out walking with a group of people, including Tycho's uncle Joergen. While crossing a bridge, the king slipped and fell into the water, and Joergen, along with others, jumped in to pull him out. The king recovered, but Tycho's uncle caught a chill, and died in June 1565. Tycho immediately came into his inheritance, and there was nothing anybody could do to stop him choosing his own career. He decided to go to Germany and study chemistry, medicine and astrology.

A nose for danger

A few days after his twentieth birthday, Tycho had a quarrel with a fellow Danish student. The two of them fought a duel with swords, and although neither of them was seriously hurt, a wild blow from his opponent's sword cut away a chunk of Tycho's nose, making a notch in the upper part. For the rest of his life, Tycho wore a special covering of gold and silver to hide the disfigurement.

Duelling injuries and scars were often carried with great pride. Some duellists would even go as far as rubbing white wine into a healing sword cut to ensure that they were left with a heroic scar.

A new star

Tycho graduated in 1568 and, soon after that, came the news that his father had died, leaving all his property to him and his brother. Tycho was now even more wealthy and independent.

The next year, in November 1572, an amazing thing happened. Tycho was walking home late one afternoon in the dark, when he noticed that something strange had happened to the W-shaped constellation known as Cassiopeia . . . there was an extra star in it that hadn't been there before!

Night after night, Tycho used his best instruments to measure the position of the new star and see if it

The further north you go, the earlier it gets dark in winter. In Sweden in November the Sun sets at about 4.00 p.m.

What Tycho saw was a supernova, a star exploding at the end of its life.

moved like a comet or a planet. It didn't. It really *was* a star, and it stayed visible for a year and a half, becoming so bright you could even see it in daylight before it finally faded away and disappeared. This was an amazing discovery that shattered the old idea of the heavens as perfect, eternal and unchanging. If a new star could appear and disappear, that meant the heavens could change. And if the heavens could change, what else might happen?

Of course, Tycho wasn't the only person to notice the bright new star, and superstitious people read all kinds of meanings into its appearance. But Tycho wrote a serious book about it, called *De Stella Nova* (*The New Star*), which gave astronomers a new word, 'nova', for a star that suddenly flares up into extreme brightness. The book made Tycho famous, and the star he saw is still often referred to as 'Tycho's star'.

Incredibly, Tycho made all his observations without the help of a telescope. This would not be used widely until the next century.

Royal Favour

Still only twenty-nine, Tycho found himself showered with gifts and fame. The king gave him a good pension and, even better, a little three-mile-long island on which to build a house and observatory. How could he refuse?

Worthy, but dull!

Tycho became a bit of a celebrity and distinguished visitors would sometimes come by boat to the island. One of these was James VI of Scotland.

Living on an island might sound fun, but most of Tycho's time was actually spent making detailed observations and calculations. For the next twenty years he continued his painstaking work – he was totally dedicated to his task.

Even Tycho still didn't get the workings of the Solar System completely right. He came up with an idea halfway between the old belief that the Earth was the centre of the Universe, and Copernicus's revolutionary theory that the Sun was at the centre. Tycho put the Earth at the centre, with the Sun and Moon orbiting round it, but all the other planets orbiting round the Sun. This model was easier for people of the time to accept.

Homeless!

The old king died in 1588 when his heir, King Christian, was only eleven. When Christian grew up, Tycho quarrelled with him and Christian decided to cut off Tycho's pension. In a huff Tycho upped sticks and set off on his travels again. He ended up in Prague, where he would live out the rest of his days. In October 1601, he suffered a stroke one night at dinner. Ten days later he died, but not before he bequeathed his astronomical data to his talented assistant, Johannes Kepler.

Johannes Kepler

Kepler's background could not have been more different from that of his privileged master, Tycho. In fact, it's a wonder he survived his childhood at all.

Kepler was born in Germany, in December 1571. His drunkard father, Heinrich, left home to become a mercenary soldier when little Johannes was just two years old. His mother, Katherine, a quarrelsome and difficult woman, decided to follow him, and the little boy was left in the care of his grandfather. While his parents were away, little Johannes caught smallpox, which affected his eyes so badly that he would never

Smallpox is a serious and sometimes fatal infectious disease. It existed for many hundreds of years, until vaccination was introduced in the twentieth century.

be able to make accurate observations of the stars and planets for himself.

Kepler's parents returned in 1576, but four years later Heinrich went off to the wars again and never came back. Katherine was left to cope alone with Johannes and his baby brother. She knew a lot about herbal medicine and had a reputation as a kind of folk healer, but even so, there was very little money coming into the household.

Despite these early setbacks, Johannes was a clever boy and managed to get a scholarship to school. He learnt Latin and did so well, even though he was often ill, that when he was seventeen he was sent to university to train to become a Lutheran (Protestant) priest.

Secret science and a new job

Kepler had always had a sneaking interest in astronomy, ever since he had seen a comet and an eclipse of the Moon when he was a child.

At university, Kepler also learnt physics, mathematics and astronomy. But this was a religious school that rejected Copernicus's outrageous idea that the planets moved round the Sun. Kepler's astronomy professor was careful only to teach the approved view that Earth was at the centre of the Universe. However, he secretly told his cleverest students, including Kepler, about the Copernican system. Kepler immediately saw how the idea made sense.

Working life

These discussions were interrupted when, luckily, Kepler landed the job of Professor of Mathematics at a religious school in Graz. He hadn't yet finished his studies and he was only twenty-two. Unfortunately, because of his age, they decided they would only pay him three-quarters of his salary until he proved his worth. Kepler was desperate for cash, so he decided to make some money on the side by casting horoscopes for the rich people of the city.

kepler's universe

In his spare time, Kepler wrote a book and fell in love. His book was called *Mysterium Cosmographicum* (*The Mystery of the Universe*) and it described his own version of the Copernican system. This was daring to the point of being quite dangerous. Luckily for Kepler, the authorities were still tolerant enough at this time not to punish him.

Although there were a lot of flaws in his work, Kepler did notice something very important. He realized that the outer planets travelled round the Sun more slowly than the inner planets did. He figured that there must be some force that moved them, which became weaker the further you got from the Sun. This was the first suggestion that there was a *physical* cause for the motion of the planets.

Kepler's book was published in 1597, in the same year that he married a young widow. They had a difficult time – two of their babies died (they later had three more children) and, as well as this, they had very little money to live on.

But despite his personal difficulties, Kepler believed totally in his work and sent copies of his book to all the top astronomers in Europe, including Tycho Brahe. The veteran astronomer was in Germany on his travels at the time and was so impressed by the book that he wrote back asking if Kepler would be interested in joining his team of assistants. Kepler didn't act straight away, but the offer would soon save him from disaster.

In fact, Kepler thought astrology was complete rubbish. He said it was 'silly and empty' and described his customers as 'fatheads'. But he made good money from telling people things they wanted to hear!

Many people believed that the planets were moved along by angels. Kepler thought that the movements were more like the workings of a clock and were nothing to do with a divine being.

political turmoil

Life could be very complicated in Europe at the end of the sixteenth century. Much of it was part of what was called the Holy Roman Empire. This wasn't really one country, but a collection of lots of little countries, ruled by various princes and dukes. Some were Catholic and some were Protestant, and wars between them were being fought all the time. Graz, where Kepler worked, was part of a small country called Styria that was ruled by Catholics. Conditions for Protestants were bearable until a new ruler, Archduke Ferdinand, came along in 1596 and made life very difficult for them. So, in 1599, when Kepler heard that Tycho was setting up an observatory at Benatky (about 300 kilometres away), he decided a visit to Tycho's home in Prague would be in order.

Escape to Tycho

Surprisingly, fifty-three-year-old Tycho was not very welcoming to Kepler at first. He had become suspicious that the younger man wanted to get his hands on his observations and use them for his own glory. Kepler was desperate to leave Graz and couldn't understand why the wealthy Tycho didn't sort things out straight away.

In the end Tycho came round. Despite his initial misgivings, he realized that Kepler was the best mathematician around, and he would be a valuable employee. Tycho offered to pay for Kepler's expenses when moving his family from Graz, and promised him that Emperor Rudolph II would give him a paid job as Tycho's assistant.

The offer came in the nick of time. Back in Graz things had got even worse. In the summer of 1600,

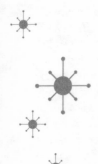

all non-Catholics were ordered to convert at once, or get out, leaving all their property behind. Kepler and his family fled, arriving in Prague in the autumn. They were little more than refugees. It was an incredibly difficult winter, but at last, in 1601, the emperor officially appointed Kepler as Tycho's assistant and put him on the payroll.

Kepler's job was enormous. He had to put all of Tycho's many thousands of observations in order, and help him publish a new set of tables of planetary positions – these were to be called the Rudolphine Tables, after the emperor.

TYcho's heir

But within a few months Tycho was dead. On his deathbed, in front of witnesses, Tycho handed over the responsibility for his vast wealth of observations, and for completing the Rudolphine Tables, to Kepler.

Kepler was appointed as Imperial Mathematician in Tycho's place. In the space of just a year, he had gone from being a penniless refugee to being the most important astronomer in Europe.

The new astronomy

Before tackling the Rudolphine Tables, there was an even more important job Kepler wanted to do. He believed that Tycho's observations should make it possible to work out the exact shape of the orbits of the planets round the Sun.

This was an enormous task. A lot of Kepler's papers still exist and they are covered with hundreds of incredibly tedious handwritten calculations. Today, it would take just a few minutes for a computer to do. But in the early seventeenth century, every number had to be worked out on paper, and

Even Copernicus had realized that the orbits couldn't be perfect circles, but this idea was rejected by the religious authorities. Circles were regarded as perfect and divine shapes, and it was believed that God would not have created anything less than perfect.

*The Rudolphine
Tables were
published in
1627. They
were thirty times
more accurate in
predicting the
movement of
the planets than
Copernicus's
tables.*

checked again and again for mistakes in all the
adding up, subtracting, multiplying and dividing. It
took years. But at last, in 1605, Kepler proved that
Mars moves in an ellipse round the Sun, and that all
the other planets move in elliptical orbits as well.
This is now known as one of 'Kepler's laws'.

Tragically for Kepler, after all that mind-numbing
work, nobody took much notice, even when his
findings were published in a book, *Astronomia
Nova*, in 1609. It wasn't until Isaac Newton used
Kepler's results to work out his own theory of
gravity nearly eighty years later that people realized
just how important this discovery was. But for
Kepler, life went on. As ever, he was constantly beset
by problems.

Wives, Witches and Wanderings

The year 1611 was a terrible one for Kepler. First,
one of his children died of smallpox. Then the
emperor went mad, and Kepler decided it would be
better to get out of Prague and find a job elsewhere.
During his search, his wife died of typhus. Kepler
eventually moved to the city of Linz, where, during
the next few years, he remarried and went on to have
six more children (only three survived).

His world was thrown into more turmoil in 1615
when his mother, Katherine, living in the German
town of Leonberg, was accused of witchcraft. This
was no joke. People convicted of witchcraft were
burnt alive, and Kepler's mother, with her skills in
herbal remedies, had turned into a cantankerous old
woman regarded with deep suspicion by her
neighbours.

*In 1615, there
was a surge of
witch-hunting in
Leonberg, and
six women were
burnt at the
stake.*

Thankfully, Kepler's mother was never actually
convicted, although she was imprisoned for

witchcraft. She was saved from anything worse by the efforts of her son, who constantly spoke up for her to the authorities.

Final years

In spite of all this, Kepler kept on with his work and published a great book, *Epitome of Copernican Astronomy* (1618–21), which boldly made the case for a Sun-centred Universe.

To add to Kepler's troubles, in 1618 the conflict between Protestants and Catholics (known as the Thirty Years War) broke out. The following year any chance he might have had of going back to Prague disappeared when Ferdinand II (already known for persecuting Protestants) became Holy Roman Emperor. Then, for once, Kepler had a relatively lucky break. In 1628 he was appointed as a personal astrologer to a duke, and the family moved to the German town of Sagan.

In 1630, Kepler was on his way back to Linz to collect some earnings he was owed, when he was struck down by a terrible fever. He died on 15 November, a month before his fifty-ninth birthday.

Barriers to scientific progress

It's amazing that Kepler achieved so much in the circumstances. His experiences show how difficult it was to be a

scientist in a war-torn Europe divided by religion. Scientists generally had a better time in England, even with a civil war raging.

The other place you might expect science to flourish in the seventeenth century was Italy, where the Renaissance had started in the previous century. But progress there was stifled when the powerful Roman Catholic Church took against some of the new ideas. The story of Galileo Galilei shows just how dangerous science could be.

Galileo Galilei

1564 was a good year for geniuses. In Stratford, England, William Shakespeare was born, while in Pisa, Italy, Galileo Galilei made his entrance into the world. He would one day become one of the world's most influential – and controversial – scientists.

Like his father, Galileo proved to be a talented musician. He was particularly good on the lute – an instrument similar to a guitar, with sixteen strings.

Galileo Galilei (known simply as Galileo) was born to Vincenzio and Giulia, a professional musician and his young wife. He was the eldest of seven children.

When Galileo was about two, his father was appointed Court Musician to the duke of Tuscany, and the entire family moved to Florence. It must have been an amazing life for the little boy. He was educated at home – mainly by his father, who was also a keen mathematician – and his family mixed with dukes and princes, artists, musicians, poets and great thinkers.

At university, Galileo was notoriously argumentative, earning him the nickname 'the wrangler'.

When Galileo was eleven he was sent to a monastery to continue his education. But the impressionable boy decided that he wanted to become a monk. His father was horrified and whisked him back to Florence, where he remained until he was seventeen.

Like many parents, Vincenzio wanted his son to have a secure profession (unlike his own job) so he then sent Galileo back to Pisa to learn how to be a doctor. But young Galileo had other ideas. In 1583, he met the court mathematician Ostilio Ricci and had a fascinating conversation with him about mathematics. He decided he would much rather be a mathematician than a medic. Vincenzio refused to let Galileo change his course, but the strong-willed boy went against his father's wishes. He promptly gave up medicine and went to maths lectures instead. In 1585, he left Pisa without taking a degree.

Falling objects

It was while he was at university that Galileo started to think about something that the Greek philosopher Aristotle once said. He was talking about hailstones and he reckoned that heavier hailstones would fall faster than smaller, lighter ones. Galileo pondered this and decided it could not be right.

There is a famous story that Galileo dropped balls of different weights from the Leaning Tower while he was in Pisa, to prove that Aristotle was wrong and they all fell at the same rate, but this is only a legend. Galileo never did the experiment.

When Galileo returned to Florence he had to scrape a living as a private tutor of maths. But he had gained enough of a reputation to be

In 1586, Simon Stevin, a Flemish engineer, did carry out this experiment from a ten-metre-high tower. Galileo may have read Stevin's results of this experiment, which showed that the balls landed at the same time.

Much later, in 1612, somebody else did the experiment to try to prove that Aristotle had been right and Galileo was wrong. The two weights really did hit the ground very nearly together. The small difference could be explained by wind resistance.

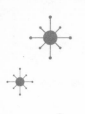

appointed Professor of Mathematics in Pisa in 1589. Although it sounds grand, it was a very poorly paid job.

A Change of Fortune

Then, in 1592, Galileo moved on to Padua, where he was paid a very respectable 180 crowns a year as Professor of Mathematics, and where he established his reputation as a leading scientist and engineer.

Galileo enjoyed a good life in Padua, and by the time he was forty it must have seemed he was settled for good. But in 1604, his life changed.

In fact, the telescope had been invented by an Englishman, Leonard Digges, in the 1550s, but he had kept it secret.

That year, another supernova (like the one Tycho had witnessed) appeared in the skies over Europe. Galileo was greatly inspired by the phenomenon and turned his attention to astronomy for the first time, giving lectures about his observations of the new star.

Stargazing

Galileo's interest gained momentum when, in 1609, rumours about a new invention from the Netherlands reached Italy – the telescope.

When Galileo heard about this amazing device – which used two lenses in a tube to make distant objects visible – he immediately built one of his own, which turned out to be better than the original prototype. He even ground his own glass lenses, which shows just how skilful he was.

The 'stars' that Galileo saw orbiting Jupiter are now known as the Galilean moons or satellites. They are: Callisto, Europa, Ganymede and Io.

Galileo's telescope was a sensation. He gave one to the Doge (Duke) of Venice, who immediately appreciated its value to a seafaring nation. But the biggest discovery came when Galileo turned a telescope on the heavens. He saw that the band of white light across the sky, known as the Milky Way, is actually made up of thousands and thousands of individual stars, too faint to be seen separately with the naked eye. And he saw four little 'stars' (actually moons) orbiting round the planet Jupiter.

Galileo had proved that there were objects in the heavens that did not revolve round the Earth. This was powerful evidence that Copernicus had been right.

At the age of forty-six, Galileo had finally made the big time. He was given the post of Chief Mathematician at the University of Pisa, and was made Philosopher and Mathematician to the grand duke of Tuscany for life.

All roads lead to Rome

In 1611, Galileo took a telescope with him on a visit to Rome, where a team of Jesuit priests made observations and officially confirmed his discovery. They were careful not to say anything about the orbits of the planets. But on a later visit to Rome, in 1615, he got an unexpectedly hostile reception. The Pope's advisers stated that the Copernican system was 'foolish and absurd . . . and formally heretical'. That meant you could be burnt at the stake if you believed in it.

This wasn't what the fifty-one-year-old Galileo had been hoping to hear. The church authorities literally would not believe the evidence of their own eyes. Nevertheless, he had to take what they said seriously.

Papal persecution

The Pope more or less said that Galileo must stop believing that the Earth orbited the Sun and that the Earth moved through space, and that he could not tell anyone that these ideas were true. But crucially, Galileo was not forbidden to *teach* people the Copernican system. He had permission from the Pope to describe it to students, or anyone else, as long as he didn't say it was true.

In 1621, the Pope died, closely followed two years later by his successor. The next Pope after that, Urban VIII, gave permission for Galileo to write a book about the Ptolemaic system and the Copernican system, on the condition that he only *described* the two models. But Galileo got carried away.

The book, called *Dialogo sopra i due massimi sistemi del mondo* (*Dialogue on the Two Chief World Systems*), was written in Italian, not Latin, and published in 1632, when Galileo was sixty-eight. It had been delayed by various problems, including an outbreak of plague in Italy.

The conversation in the book is between two fictional characters, Salviati and Simplicio; Salviati presents the Copernican system and Simplicio presents the Ptolemaic

One of Galileo's crimes was that he had 'dared' to write his book in Italian, so that ordinary people could understand it

system. The trouble was that anyone who read the book could tell that Salviati wins the debate. Worse, the name Simplicio gives the idea that anyone, like the Pope, who believes the Ptolemaic idea that the Earth is at the centre of the Universe, must be a bit simple-minded.

Not surprisingly, the Pope was furious, and Galileo was summoned to Rome to face trial for heresy. One of his 'crimes' was that he had praised William Gilbert, who supported the Copernican system and was regarded by the Catholic Church as a heretic.

At his trial, Galileo was found guilty. He was threatened with torture and forced to 'confess' that all his ideas were wrong. He was lucky not to be sentenced to death, but was instead forced to spend the rest of his life under house arrest at his villa near Florence.

Final years

Here, Galileo secretly wrote another book, known as *Two New Sciences*, summing up everything he had learnt in his long lifetime, and promoting the scientific method of doing experiments pioneered by Gilbert. The manuscript was smuggled out of Italy and published in the Netherlands, in 1638. The book had a big influence on the growth of science everywhere – except in Italy. Because of the way Galileo had been treated, many people were afraid of making scientific investigations here and it took a long time for the country to recover from this setback.

By the time the book was published, the elderly Galileo had gone blind. Yet still he worked on, helped by his son and his assistant. But just a few weeks before his seventy-eighth birthday, in February 1642, Galileo died quietly in his sleep.

At the time Galileo died, a fifteen-year-old boy from Ireland was visiting Florence. The sensational arguments stirred up

By using a dialogue to explain his ideas, Galileo was following a method often used by ancient scholars to help students understand a complex problem. It was also a neat way of teaching his 'heretical' ideas without actually endorsing them.

It wasn't until 350 years after Galileo's death that the Catholic Church granted him an official pardon

by news of the great man's death intrigued the boy and he was determined to find out more. He began reading everything he could about Galileo and his work, and started on the path that would make him a great scientist as well. His name was Robert Boyle, and he was one of two Roberts who would help to make England the centre of the scientific world in the second half of the seventeenth century.

Chapter Five

The Two Roberts

The Two Roberts

Two men, both called Robert, who were both great experimenters of the seventeenth century. The first Robert transformed magical alchemy into proper chemistry. The second used a new invention – the microscope – to literally open people's eyes up to the world around them.

Robert Boyle

Boyle's ideas about air, atoms and alchemy were often way ahead of his time.

Born into riches

The famous school Eton is renowned for its sporting traditions, even having its own games, such as Eton Fives (a bit like tennis without the racquets) and the Eton Wall game (a type of football). They are still played to this day.

Born in County Waterford, Ireland, on 25 January 1627, Robert was the youngest boy in the family. He was the fourteenth child of Richard Boyle, Earl of Cork, the richest man in the British Isles.

Although his father was very wealthy, Robert certainly didn't have an easy childhood. Strict Earl Richard didn't believe in 'spoiling' children, and when Robert was still just a baby he was sent away to live with another family to 'toughen him up'. Poor little Robert never saw his mother again, as she died when he was only four.

Robert returned home when he was five and was given a basic education in reading, writing, Latin and French. Three years later, he was sent away again, this time to school in England. Surprisingly, Robert, who was never a healthy person, loved the harsh academic life at Eton – but he hated having to leave his lessons to play sport and games.

When Robert was twelve, his father sent him, his older brother Francis and a tutor on a grand tour of Europe. Francis, aged fifteen, was somewhat miffed by this directive from his father; just four days earlier he had been married to the beautiful Elizabeth Stafford, and didn't want to leave his new bride.

The trip took several years and in 1651, when Robert was fourteen, he found himself in Florence at the exact same time that Galileo died. His interest in science was fired by all the fuss about the death of the great man, and inspired him to read all of Galileo's works.

The grand tour, visiting all of Europe's ancient and cultural sites, was considered just the thing to educate a rich young gentleman, right up until the early twentieth century.

Rebellion and war

But while Francis and Robert were enjoying themselves in Europe, a rebellion against the English broke out in Ireland, and the earl lost almost his entire fortune in the conflict. Two of the boys' brothers died in the fighting, and the earl himself died in 1643.

Francis was old enough to hurry back to help, but Robert was told to stay where he was. Unfortunately, the allowance from his father dried up, and when he did eventually return to England in 1644, Robert was virtually penniless and heavily in debt to his tutor. To make matters worse, England was in the middle of the civil war.

Robert had the good sense to keep as far away from the trouble as possible, and went to live quietly in a small house in Dorset left to him by his father. It was here that he started carrying out scientific experiments in earnest. He also made visits to London to see his sister Katherine, and began to meet other scientists through her.

A change in fortune

Boyle's law is important to SCUBA divers, who breathe air from pressurized tanks when they are deep underwater. The pressure of this air stops their lungs being squashed by the pressure of the water.

Things calmed down in Ireland when the civil war was over, and in 1652 Robert went back there for two years to sort out some of the mess his father's estates had been left in. He managed to secure an income of £3,000 a year for the rest of his life – that's like having a million pounds a year today. Such a massive fortune meant he could do anything he wanted, so in 1654 he moved to Oxford, the centre of scientific activity in England at the time, with the idea of becoming a real scientist.

Being extremely rich, Boyle didn't have to bother with getting a degree. He just set up his own laboratory in Oxford and hired a team of assistants to help him with his work.

The air that we breathe

Boyle was fascinated by air. He measured the 'springiness' of air; he messed around with vacuums and tried to discover what air was made of. In one of his most famous experiments he poured mercury into a J-shaped tube sealed at the short end. This left a pocket of air trapped in the short arm of the J, between the mercury and the seal. He then poured more mercury in, squeezing the air pocket into a smaller space. He found that if you double the pressure on the air, you halve the amount of space (volume) it takes up. Boyle's discovery is known as Boyle's law, which says, in science speak, that the volume of a gas is inversely proportional to pressure.

Experiments with vacuums

A vacuum is a space in which all or most of the air has been pumped out. Boyle created vacuums using a special device that pumped air out of glass containers.

Together, Boyle and his assistant did experiments to find out what can and can't exist in a vacuum. They found out that nothing will burn in a vacuum, that sound doesn't travel in a vacuum and, more importantly, that animals cannot live in a vacuum. They discovered this by putting small animals and birds into the glass vessel and pumping out the air. Of course, the unfortunate creatures died.

Boyle described all his discoveries about air in a book published in 1660, in English, called *The Spring of the Air*.

The air pump was developed by one of Boyle's assistants, Robert Hooke, the other Robert of this chapter.

Alchemy v chemistry

In Boyle's time, there were still people who thought you could turn other (base) metals into gold, essentially by magic. This study was called alchemy. Boyle did more than anyone to transform alchemy into proper chemistry.

Alchemists believed you could make gold by taking the impurities out of metals such as copper or silver. But gold is denser than these other metals. In other words, a piece of gold will be heavier than a piece of silver or copper of the same size. Boyle argued that if you took out the impurities, the metal would get lighter, not heavier, so it must be impossible to make gold in this way. He was right.

Like modern chemists, Boyle realized how important it was to do careful and accurate experiments, instead of just throwing in a handful of this and a few drops of something else to see what happened. His ideas were published in *The Sceptical Chymist*, in 1661.

Boyle's experiments with animals may seem barbaric to us. But remember this was a crueller time than today. People were still burnt at the stake and the rights of animals simply weren't considered.

Ahead of his time

Up until Boyle, most people still believed in the old Greek idea that everything was made of the four 'elements': air, earth, fire and water. Boyle made a huge leap in our understanding by saying instead that everything is made up of tiny particles, called atoms. These atoms are joined together in different ways to make the variety of things we see around us. Boyle thought that atoms must move about easily in liquids and gases, which is why they have no shape, but are motionless in solids. All these ideas were way ahead of their time, and nobody else developed them for decades.

The Greek philosopher Democritus (c.460 BC–c.370 BC) had been the first to suggest the idea of atoms, but his theory was not as well-developed as Boyle's and it had never caught on.

A Royal Society

Amazingly, science still carried on during the terrible upheaval of the civil war and fared reasonably well even during Oliver Cromwell's time in charge of the country. It was at this time that a group of scientists from Oxford got together with another group of thinkers in London and organized themselves into a proper society. When King Charles II was restored in 1660, his interest in science gave the group the backing they needed. In 1662, the society received a royal charter and officially became the Royal Society.

Boyle published his ideas about atoms in Origin of Forms and Qualities, *in 1666.*

Boyle moved to London in 1668, when he was forty-one, to live with his sister. He continued his scientific work at his own laboratory in Katherine's house, but his great days of discovery were over. Katherine died just before Christmas 1690, and a week later, Boyle finally succumbed to the poor health that had dogged him all his life, dying on 30 December.

By this time the Royal Society was well established as the leading scientific organization in

The Royal Society soon became the most important scientific organization in the world. Boyle was one of its founder members.

the world. This was largely thanks to the other Robert, Boyle's former assistant, Robert Hooke. For all his other achievements, it could be said that Boyle's greatest discovery was Hooke himself.

Boyle was described as very tall, straight, virtuous, frugal and charitable, a great and good man, but so frail that he seemed as delicate as glass.

Robert Hooke

> Probably one of the most underrated scientists ever, it is only in more recent times that we have realized how great Robert Hooke's contribution was to the worlds of science and architecture.

Like Kepler, Robert Hooke was very poor compared to his wealthy master. He was born in 1635, in Freshwater on the Isle of Wight, the son of a curate (a kind of vicar's assistant). A curate in those days received a measly salary, so Robert and his brother and sister had a very poor upbringing. Robert was also a sickly child, and it was a great surprise to his parents that he survived at all.

There seemed little point in spending hard-earned money sending frail Robert to school, so his father taught him at home. But most of the time Robert was left on his own to do what he liked.

Hooke recollected that for the first seven years of his life he lived entirely on milk and fruit, because anything else made him sick.

And what he liked doing was making things. Robert was so good with his hands that when he was about ten or twelve years old he made a beautiful model ship, about a metre long, with all its sails and rigging, and with tiny guns that actually fired. When he was given an old brass clock to play with, he took it to bits and made copies of all the pieces, creating a working clock out of wood.

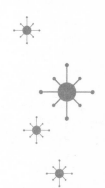

Artistic ambitions

In those days, you needed an apprenticeship – learning your trade while working for someone more experienced than you – to get into certain professions. Hooke was originally apprenticed to the great portrait painter of the time, Sir Peter Lely.

When a famous artist, John Hoskins, came to Freshwater, young Hooke carefully watched what he did, made his own paints out of whatever came to hand, and started copying paintings. He was so good that his family thought he might make a living as an artist. When his father died in 1648, thirteen-year-old Robert received an inheritance of £100. Robert decided to go to London to become a painter. But the reality of being an artist didn't quite match up to the dream. Not only was an apprenticeship incredibly expensive, Robert then realized that the smell of paints made him ill – so he gave it up.

Hooke then decided that what he really needed was an education. His inheritance and a good word from the vicar of Freshwater got him into Westminster School. One of his fellow pupils was Christopher Wren, who went on to become a great architect. Hooke would one day work with him.

Hooke had a deformed back, and he believed that it was the many hours he had spent hunched over his woodworking tools that gave him this twisted appearance.

Hooke got on incredibly well at school, being so bright he hardly ever had to attend his lessons in Latin, Greek and maths. He much preferred to go off to the workshops attached to the school, talking to the craftsmen there and making things.

Off to university

Hooke won a scholarship to go to Christ Church, Oxford, in 1653. Talent like Hooke's couldn't stay hidden for long, and several of the professors at the university asked him to help them with their experiments. This is how he became Robert Boyle's chief assistant.

Hooke made the air pump for Robert Boyle, and the two of them carried out dozens of experiments together using it. Just how important Hooke was to

Boyle is shown by the fact that Boyle named him in his book. This would never have happened unless Hooke was incredibly talented. The aristocratic Boyle was careful to pick out the man who was his equal in scientific terms, if not socially, for special mention.

Today Boyle and Hooke would be regarded as equal partners in their research – and Boyle's law would more properly be known as the Boyle–Hooke law – but in the seventeenth century, money and patronage were everything.

A practical solution

The gentlemen scientists of the Royal Society had a problem. They were all very clever, and very interested in science, but none of them was any good at practical things; they couldn't make the equipment they needed for their experiments or demonstrate their new discoveries. They needed someone who could do all this for them. They needed Hooke!

Boyle recommended Robert Hooke for the job – Curator of Experiments – and in 1662 Hooke left Oxford to take up the post in London. He never finished his degree, but in 1663 the university awarded him an MA anyway, and the Royal Society elected him as one of its Fellows. Not bad for a poor boy from Freshwater.

In 1665, just before his thirtieth birthday, Hooke became Professor of Geometry at Gresham College, where the Royal Society also had its rooms. This meant that as well as the financial security (it was a job for life) he was able to live above the Royal Society, and could carry out his duties more easily.

The Society made Hooke work very hard indeed, carrying out all kinds of experiments for the Fellows,

By the standards of his day, Boyle was being extremely generous in acknowledging Hooke's contribution.

Over the next forty years, it was Hooke, more than anybody else, who turned the Royal Society into a proper scientific organization. Without him, it would have been just a fashionable club where gentlemen could meet to chat over a cup of coffee.

and demonstrating five or six different things at each of the weekly meetings. Unfortunately, the funds were not always available for them to pay his salary promptly. Luckily for Hooke, he was kept solvent by generous handouts from Boyle.

The magic of the microscope

Amateur Leeuwenhoek identified tiny living creatures in water (protozoa and bacteria), which he called 'animalcules' and made the first accurate description of red blood cells.

On top of all this, Hooke was also doing his own experiments. At this time, he was very interested in the new science of microscopy.

People like Galileo made microscopes as well as telescopes. They used two lenses mounted in a tube to magnify things. But other early scientists used very small single lenses to do the same job. The expert with this kind of microscope was a Dutchman called Antoni van Leeuwenhoek. The kind of microscope Galileo used would magnify things thirty times. But van Leeuwenhoek used a tiny spherical lens, which magnified things 300 times. The trouble was, it was very difficult to use these tiny lenses, so people stopped using them when better multiple-lens microscopes were invented. They are called compound microscopes.

The fact that Micrographia was so readable made it seem as if his work were easy, and people of the time never quite realized just how skilful and talented Hooke was.

Hooke made significant improvements to the compound microscope and, remarkably, his basic design has hardly changed in over 350 years. His microscopes look remarkably similar to the ones you probably use in science lessons at school. Hooke's microscopes allowed him to see remarkable detail. He wrote the first book about what could be seen, and illustrated it with beautiful and accurate drawings that he had done himself.

It was called *Micrographia*, and was published by the Royal Society in 1665. The book was written in English, and became hugely popular.

The famous diarist Samuel Pepys (who was also a Fellow of the Royal Society) described in his diary how he got hold of one of the first copies of the book and was so enthralled that he sat up all night reading it by candlelight. He said it was 'the most ingenious book that I ever read in my life'.

plague! Fire!

Soon after *Micrographia* was published, the plague hit London. Like anyone else who could get out of the city, Hooke moved away while the disease raged.

Things had barely got back to normal in London when, on Sunday, 2 September 1666, the Great Fire broke out, and much of the city was destroyed. Science had to take a back seat in Hooke's life for the next few years, because he was appointed to work alongside Christopher Wren, another Fellow of the Royal Society, who was in charge of the rebuilding of the city.

Rebuilding London

Most history books tell you that Christopher Wren designed the new street plans and the many beautiful churches that rose from the ashes. They don't mention Hooke. But the two men were more or less equal partners in this work and many of the 'Wren' churches that people admire today were actually designed by Hooke. He also worked with Wren in laying out the pattern of streets that has survived to the present day.

It was hard work, but rewarding. Hooke earned several thousand pounds, which made him a rich man for the rest of his life. But he always lived frugally, never married, and when he died he left

Bubonic plague, a normally fatal infection, is spread through flea bites. It was brought to England from Europe by rat fleas on a boat docking in Weymouth, in 1348. Outbreaks were common for more than 300 years.

The Great Fire of London destroyed a huge area of the city, including eighty-seven churches and 13,200 houses. Incredibly, only six people are known to have died. The fire started in the king's baker's shop, in Pudding Lane near London Bridge.

£10,000 in cash (more than a million pounds in today's money) in a locked chest in his room.

A new talent emerges

In the 1670s, most of the hard work involved in planning the rebuilding of London was over. Hooke could now properly concentrate on his scientific work again. Just at this time, the Royal Society heard about a young man in Cambridge, Isaac Newton, who had invented a new kind of telescope.

Newton, who was seven years younger than Hooke, was a newcomer to the scientific scene. The Royal Society was so impressed by his telescope that they made Newton a Fellow, and were eager to find out what else he had been working on. This simple request led to one of the biggest rows in science, and to a famous remark that most people have misunderstood for more than 300 years.

A light argument

Newton sent the Royal Society a paper describing his ideas about light and colour: things such as rainbows and how light bends when it passes through a glass prism. The work was impressively good, and much of it was new science. But some of it was based on Hooke's experiments that he had described in *Micrographia*, and Newton hadn't made this clear.

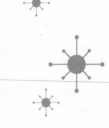

Hooke was pretty annoyed. He felt that Newton was trying to pretend that *he* had discovered the things Hooke had discovered. He was especially cross because Newton was a younger man whom nobody had ever heard of, who, quite frankly, should have had more respect for his elders.

The trouble was, Newton had no respect for anybody. He knew how clever he was, and didn't think anybody else was fit to lick his boots in the world of science. He simply didn't care if Hooke was upset. The two of them had a huge row, mostly by letter. In the end, the Royal Society had to do something about it – the Society was becoming the laughing stock of London.

They insisted that Hooke and Newton write to each other apologizing and burying the hatchet. Hooke swallowed his pride and wrote just the kind of letter the Royal Society wanted: 'Your design and mine, are, I suppose, both at the same thing, which is the discovery of truth,' wrote Hooke, slightly grudgingly.

Hooke also made the point that if it hadn't been for the Great Fire of London, and all his work with Wren, he would probably have carried on with the work he described in *Micrographia*, and gone on to make some of the discoveries Newton made.

Newton always thought he was better than anybody, including the Ancient Greeks.

A famous remark

Newton also wrote a letter. In it he praised Hooke's work and added that if he had seen further than Hooke, it was by 'standing on the shoulders of Giants'. This was a fairly common expression and it was usually meant as a tribute to the learning of the Ancient Greeks, in the days when people thought they were only rediscovering things the Greeks had known centuries before.

People thought Newton must have been very modest to give so much credit to the Ancients. But he wasn't! Remember that Hooke was a little man with a twisted back. By choosing that particular phrase, and putting a capital G on Giants, it is more than likely that Newton was saying to Hooke, 'I don't need to steal ideas from a weedy little man like you.' It was pure Newton nastiness, and very typical of him.

After the exchange of letters, Newton declared to his friends that he would never publish anything else about light while Hooke was alive. True to his word, although he wrote a great book about light, called *Opticks*, he waited until Hooke died in 1703, and published it the next year, when Hooke couldn't answer back. His plan was so successful that to this day one of the important discoveries Hooke describes in *Micrographia* is known as 'Newton's rings'.

For many years, Robert Hooke never received the credit that was due to him as a scientist. People in the eighteenth century were in awe of the achievements of Isaac Newton, and didn't realize how much people like Hooke had contributed to the scientific revolution. And they still thought of Hooke as being some kind of servant to the clever gentlemen of the Royal Society, a kind of lab assistant who only did what he was told by gentlemen like Robert Boyle. It was really only in the twentieth century that historians began to realize just how important Hooke was.

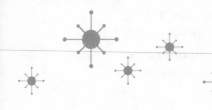

chapter six

Irresistible Forces

Isaac Newton

Made famous by a falling apple, this difficult but brilliant man turned people's thinking on its head with his amazing discoveries about the universe.

Humble beginnings

On Christmas Day 1642, the first year of the English civil war, a tiny baby was born in Woolsthorpe, Lincolnshire. Little Isaac Newton was so small that, as the man himself wrote later, he would have fitted into a 'quart pot'. He was not expected to survive.

Despite the poor outlook, Newton lived but he did not have the happiest start in life. His father, a farmer, had died three months before Isaac was born and, when he was three years old, his mother remarried. Her new husband, Barnabas Smith, wanted nothing to do with the boy, so Isaac was sent off to live with his elderly grandparents.

As an adult Newton had a habit of getting into nasty arguments with his acquaintances. Even as a child he would brood over certain incidents and plan his revenge on the offending person.

It was a miserable time. Torn away from his mother and with no brothers or sisters to play with, Newton became a lonely and reclusive child. He developed a burning hatred for the stepfather who had taken his mother away, and a few years later he would make a list of his 'sins' that included 'threatening my father and mother Smith to burn them and the house over them'. It was probably an empty threat but just mulling over this unpleasant revenge would have given Newton some sort of satisfaction.

Although Newton's grandparents were kind, they were old and not used to young children, so they decided to send him away to school – a move that

unwittingly did Newton (and science) a huge favour. It was very unusual for a boy from his background to go to school in those days. Indeed, if Newton's father had lived, Newton would most likely have followed in his footsteps and become an illiterate farmer.

Books and bullies

Newton was lonely at school, being extremely quiet, thoughtful and studious. He didn't join in with the games being played by the other boys, preferring to be alone or talk with the girls, and he became a prime target for school bullies. However, despite his quiet nature, Newton had a seething temper when roused. Once, when he was picked on by a larger boy, he beat his opponent so hard during the ensuing fight that the bully ran away. This outburst of temper – and his victory over a boy bigger than himself – meant that the other boys never tried bullying him again.

But violence wasn't the only way that Isaac Newton got his own back on bullies and the country people around him that he never liked. He terrified the superstitious locals and mystified his fellow pupils by sneaking out on dark nights to fly a hand-made kite that had a bright paper lantern attached to it. This also caused one of the earliest ever recorded UFO scares!

When Newton was eleven, his stepfather died and he went back to live with his mother on the family farm. For the time being he was allowed to continue his education. But, at the age of sixteen, his mother decided he was needed to look after the farm. Newton was hopeless. When he was supposed to be looking after the animals he would be sitting on the grass reading books, oblivious to what was going on around him. He was fined several times for letting his animals wander into other farmers' fields and damage their crops.

It was only because he was such a disaster that his mother eventually let him go to university. A family contact called Humphrey Babington had heard how clever Newton was and recommended him for a place at Trinity College, Cambridge, where he was a Fellow. An ecstatic Newton started university in 1661, the year after Charles II was restored to the throne. As Newton only had £10 a year from his mother to live on, he had to work as Babington's servant (or subsizar) to live. But since his master was hardly ever there, there was very little work to do.

Newton was lucky. The subsizar had to do all the unpleasant jobs, such as emptying their master's chamber pots.

university Challenge

There were only two universities in England in Newton's day. Oxford was probably the best place in the world to study science in the 1660s. But although Cambridge had once been one of the best universities (when it was founded in the thirteenth century), by Newton's time it had declined so much that it was, by the standards of other European universities, a backward place. At that point only a third of all the students who entered the university left with a degree, even though the only requirement for graduating was just to stay there for four years – you didn't have to be bright or hard working, you just had to be there!

Newton did eventually make one good friend. Early in 1663 he met up with a fellow student, Nicholas Wickens, and they got along so well together that they decided to share rooms, much as flatmates would today.

From what we know of Newton's life at Cambridge it seems that he had a miserable first year there. He had no friends and lost himself in solitary reading.

Incredibly, there was no teaching of science at

Cambridge, so whatever Newton learnt he learnt alone, and through his own efforts. He worked obsessively hard, a solitary thinker deep in his books. In fact, he worked so hard that he soon knew more than his professors. Rather like Archimedes, he was so devoted to study that he would forget about everything else. He would stay up all night reading books, even forgetting to eat. And, like Archimedes, when he did venture outside his rooms he could often be seen, deep in thought, drawing mathematical diagrams on the path with a stick.

ESCapiNG the plague

By 1665 Newton had graduated and was planning to stay in Cambridge, when the plague struck. The great plague, which eventually wiped out much of London's population, affected most of Europe in the 1660s and spread to many cities in Britain. In Cambridge, so many people fled from its horrors that the university had to be closed down temporarily and many students moved out to the surrounding villages, accompanied by their tutors. But as Newton worked entirely alone, and already had his degree, he decided to return home to Lincolnshire. It was a full two years before he would return to Cambridge in 1667. It was then, and particularly in 1666, that Newton did most of the scientific work for which he is now famous. He worked out his ideas about light and colour (starting from Hooke's book) and it was at this time he had his famous row with Hooke. He worked out the mathematical technique called calculus, and he

No one knows exactly why Newton kept his achievements quiet but, as he was such a secretive person, it isn't too surprising.

developed some of his revolutionary ideas about gravity. He even invented a new kind of telescope. But he didn't tell anyone.

Unlike the famous story, Newton didn't start thinking about gravity because an apple fell on his head. But he did see an apple falling from a tree and, just as importantly, he saw the Moon in the sky *above* the apple tree. This set him thinking about the force that pulled the apple down from the tree and he wondered if that same force could also reach all the way from the Earth to the Moon. He eventually proved this to be the case and, as you'll see later, the discovery of this 'universal law' would change the way people thought about the world forever.

A Change of mind

Newton had achieved most of his groundbreaking scientific work by the time he was twenty-four. But because he kept it quiet he did not achieve fame until he was forty-five.

Back in Cambridge, Newton was doing rather well. He became a Fellow of Trinity College in 1667 and Lucasian Professor of Mathematics two years later, with a decent income of £100 a year. All this meant that he could, if he wanted, spend the rest of his life in the college, studying anything he wanted. But, inexplicably, after everything he had achieved (remember, by this time he had thought up all his important scientific ideas) Newton more or less gave up science and instead turned to a new interest – alchemy, the highly *un*scientific process of trying to make gold from base metal. If it hadn't been for the encouragement of a fellow scientist, he might never have let the world know about his amazing discoveries.

A man of influence

Newton finally came out of his shell after he had a visit, in Cambridge, from a young astronomer,

Edmond Halley, in 1684. Halley had been having a friendly argument with Hooke and Christopher Wren, back in London, about planetary orbits. By then everybody knew for sure that the planets moved round the Sun in elliptical orbits. The three men guessed that there must be some influence, or force, from the Sun that was pulling on the planets to keep them in their orbits. But what kind of force?

Halley, Hooke and Wren had each worked out by themselves that any such force would have to obey something called an inverse square law. This sounds complicated but 'inverse' just means 'one over', and 'square' just means multiplying a number by itself. In other words: when a planet is twice as far away from the Sun it feels one quarter as much pull; when it is three times further away it feels one ninth as much pull, and so on.

All three men wondered if gravity might be the inverse square force that was influencing the planets. But they couldn't prove it. And they didn't know if an inverse square force was the *only* way that planets could be kept in their orbits. So Halley went to Cambridge to ask Newton for his help.

Halley was amazed when Newton told him that he had worked that puzzle out long ago. Indeed, he had actually *proved* that gravity was indeed the inverse square force that holds the planets in their orbits. No other force could do the job. But Newton had lost the papers on which he had worked it all out. He told Halley to go away and come back when he had had a chance to write it out again.

Fame beckons

Newton soon produced a beautiful nine-page paper with the proof, and also hinted that he had done

The Principia *included everything Newton knew about science, except for his work on optics – the cause of his arguments with Hooke. Newton made sure that his book* Opticks *was not published until after Hooke's death.*

other important scientific work. Impressed, Halley and the Royal Society tried to persuade him to put it all into a big book. Newton was reluctant but with Halley's encouragement the book was published in 1687. Called *Philosophiae Naturalis Principia Mathematica* (*The Mathematical Principles of Natural Philosophy*), or the *Principia* for short, it is the greatest book of science ever written.

What was so special about the *Principia*? Well, the book explained that the Universe is ruled by the same laws that rule everything on Earth, laws that ordinary people can understand. For example, the law of gravity that explains how an apple falls to the ground also explains how the Moon orbits round the Earth, how planets orbit the Sun and how other solar systems beyond ours operate. It is truly a universal law.

This turned people's thinking on its head. Before the *Principia*, people could still imagine that the heavens were in a different league to the Earth, and might be ruled by the will of God, or the gods. After the *Principia*, it was clear that the Universe is an orderly place governed by rules. It was the moment when science came of age.

The book caused a great deal of excitement and Newton became famous as a result. But, instead of doing more scientific work, he used his newfound fame to help him on the road to other successful careers unrelated to science.

New friends, new money

Newton became involved in the turbulent world of politics for the first time. In 1689, the Catholic James II was thrown out of England and replaced by the Protestant William of Orange and his wife, Mary.

King James II had been one of the two little princes who sheltered by a hedge with scientist William Harvey during the Battle of Edgehill.

Newton had been one of the old king's most outspoken opponents. When William came to the throne, Newton was elected as an MP representing Cambridge in the new Parliament.

Seven years later, in 1696, Newton was appointed as Warden of the Royal Mint, which was then based in the Tower of London. He showed himself to be an efficient and ruthless manager. He took charge of a complete recoinage of the currency (equivalent to changing over from pounds to euros in our day) in which every gold and silver coin in the country had to be called in, melted down and reissued. Newton was soon promoted to the top job, Master of the Mint.

Getting his own back

Other successes followed, including a knighthood. Then in 1703 the death of Hooke opened up another door for Newton. Ever since their famous row Newton had kept well out of his way and that also meant keeping away from the activities of the Royal Society. But once Hooke had died, Newton decided to stand for election and became President of the society just before his fifty-ninth birthday.

Before the 'meltdown', there were many forged coins in the country. Newton was responsible for sentencing the forgers – the usual punishment was death by hanging. Newton took no pleasure in inflicting such punishments but, nevertheless, he carried out his orders with a chilling efficiency.

For the rest of his life, Newton ran the Royal Society with the same ruthless efficiency that he ran the Royal Mint. The irony is that Hooke, who Newton hated, had made the Royal Society a highly regarded institution. With Newton at the helm, it became the well-run organization it is today. It needed both men, who would never have worked together, to make it work.

Seven years after Hooke's death, Newton managed to get in one last piece of petty revenge. The Royal Society was about to move from its overcrowded rooms to a new location. Newton took personal charge of the move, including the care of the many portraits that had to be taken down at Gresham College and put back up on the walls of the new building, Crane Court. Only one of the portraits was mysteriously 'lost', never to be seen again – the picture of Robert Hooke.

Unpleasant though he was in many ways, Newton was still the greatest scientist of all time. When he died, in 1727 at the age of eighty-four, he was worth £30,000, an immense fortune, and was famous throughout the civilized world. But his fame would soon rise to even greater heights, thanks to his old friend, Edmond Halley. And Halley, like Newton, was not only a great scientist but a man of many other talents and interests.

Edmond Halley

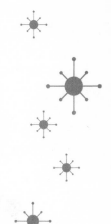

He will go down in history as the comet man but his achievements went much further. Described as being a combination of Horatio Hornblower, James Bond and Stephen Hawking, he captained a Royal Navy ship, worked as a part-time spy and made tremendous advances in our knowledge of the universe.

The boy with a silver spoon

The son of a wealthy businessman, young Edmond Halley was born in 1656 in Hackney, London. As a boy, he was sent to the best and most expensive school in the city, St Paul's, and then on to Oxford University, where he began his studies in 1673.

By this time, Halley was already a keen amateur astronomer and, thanks to his family's wealth, he had all the latest technology that money could buy. He arrived in Oxford with a 7.3 metre long telescope and many other instruments that were even better than the ones used by professional astronomers. He was so fascinated by the stars that observing the skies took up much of his time but, despite this, he still managed to be an outstanding all-round student.

Seeing stars

Two years later, when Halley was still an undergraduate, the Royal Greenwich Observatory was set up and a man called John Flamsteed was appointed as the first Astronomer Royal. The two men got to know each other and ended up becoming friends. With Flamsteed's encouragement, Halley had a paper about planetary orbits published. This success started Halley thinking about a much more adventurous idea, a way in which he could make his mark upon the world.

At Greenwich, Flamsteed was just starting an important new survey. He wanted to map the sky, showing the positions of all the bright stars. Because he would be using a telescope for the first time, this work would be much more accurate than anything done before. But only the northern sky is visible from Greenwich. Halley wondered if he could do the same kind of survey of the southern sky.

This was a daring (and expensive) idea for a young man of nineteen to come up with. But Halley was no ordinary young man. He had rich and influential friends and relatives, and he got them all involved. His father loved the idea, and promised to give him an allowance of £300 a year to do the job. Halley's good friend Flamsteed persuaded the king to let Edmond travel free on one of the Crown's ships.

And so, in November 1676, a jubilant Halley abandoned his university course and set out on the voyage with his friend James Clerke. They sailed to the most southerly of Britain's colonies, the island of St Helena in the South Atlantic and set about the task of mapping the stars. Halley returned to England in 1678 where his survey,

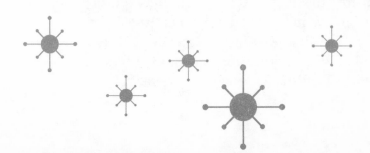

entitled the *Catalogue of the Southern Stars*, was a great success, earning him the nickname 'Our Southern Tycho'.

That wasn't all it earned him. Before the end of the year Halley, only twenty-two years old, was elected a Fellow of the Royal Society.

The king was also delighted with Halley's work and wrote to Oxford to request that Halley be awarded an MA degree by the university. They could hardly refuse.

Having achieved so much so soon, rather like a pop star after the first wave of success, Halley was quite happy to relax and enjoy himself for a while. He spent the next months hanging out in fashionable coffee houses, visiting Oxford and generally having a good time. Then he set out on the gentlemanly grand tour of Europe to complete his all-round education.

A comet is a ball of dirty ice that follows an elongated orbit around the Sun. When it is near the Sun ice evaporates from it and gases stream out behind in a 'tail'.

The First comet

Halley's grand tour began just after a comet was spotted in the sky in November 1680. It was the brightest comet that anyone alive had ever seen. A little later what was thought to be a second bright comet was seen in the skies over Europe. We now know that it was the very same comet that had travelled towards the Sun, become lost in the bright glare of sunlight, and moved round the other side of the Sun into the dark depths of space again. It was a huge topic of conversation among the people Halley met as he travelled through France and Italy, many of them top mathematicians and astronomers. But it would be another comet in the future, one

that Halley never lived to see, that he would one day become famous for.

Halley returned to London at the beginning of 1682, where he got married and settled down, still living off his father's allowance. But a family tragedy in March 1684 was to change Halley's fortunes. His father disappeared in mysterious circumstances and a few days later his body was found in the river. An inquest returned a verdict of murder but it turned out he had money problems so it was possible that he committed suicide. Halley had to fight a legal battle with his stepmother to get his share of the inheritance that remained. While this was going on he found himself in need of money for the first time in his life. In 1686 he resigned as a Fellow of the Royal Society so that he could become the paid Clerk of the Society.

Halley's new job didn't stop him keeping up his own scientific work, including research on the weather and trying to solve the problems of navigation at sea. He helped others in their work too. Halley was a key influence in bringing Newton's famous book *Principia* to the public. He helped Newton by soothing him when he got angry, he dealt with the printers for him and he even ended up paying for the book to be published!

Then, in 1691, he once again came up with an adventurous seafaring scheme.

Halley was also the first person to invent a diving bell. This allowed men to work on the sea floor at depths of up to ten fathoms (eighteen metres) for two hours at a time.

The Voyage of Captain Halley

As part of his work on navigation Halley wanted to voyage to the southern ocean to measure the magnetic field in different places, with the idea of producing a 'magnetic map' for ships. He asked the navy for help. They loved the idea, and offered to

build a small ship, known as a 'pink',
specially for the job. The ship,
named the *Paramore*, was ready
for its maiden voyage in 1696. It
was just fifty-two feet long and
eighteen feet wide. Halley was
appointed by the king, now
William III, as Master and
Commander of the *Paramore*.

Being the senior officer on the ship, Halley would
be known as the captain; commanding officers in the
navy are always called captain, whatever their rank.
This was very unusual. Halley is the only 'landsman'
ever to be appointed as Captain of a king's ship.
Some of the others, especially the first lieutenant,
Edward Harrison (who had eight years' experience),
were unhappy about Halley being in charge. The
ship embarked on its voyage with a great deal of bad
feeling among the crew.

A storm brews

By the time the *Paramore* reached the West Indies in
May 1699, the tension between Halley and Harrison
had exploded into a huge row. Harrison stormed off
to his cabin and left Halley to navigate the ship as
best he could, obviously hoping Halley would make
a total mess of it.

But navigation in those days was all about
measuring the ship's position by the stars, and
Halley, an expert astronomer, was a superb
navigator. He brought the ship back to England
successfully, where Harrison was court-martialled
for disobeying a senior officer. Then Halley went
back to sea without his troublesome lieutenant. He
voyaged as far south as 52° latitude, deep into

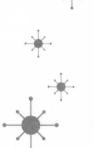

iceberg territory, and completed his observations with aplomb, returning to Plymouth in August 1700. He was promptly re-elected as a Fellow of the Royal Society.

Going Undercover

Halley was such a success as a scientific captain that the navy used him over the next few months to carry out studies of the tides in the English Channel. At least, that's what they said he was doing. Actually, as well as studying tides, Halley was secretly mapping the approaches to French harbours and spying on their harbour defences, to make charts that the navy could use if there was a war.

We know that Halley did more spying for the government, because a letter dated 14 January 1704 states that he was paid £36 'out of the secret service' fund. But nobody knows exactly what he did.

Halley achieved the pinnacle of his ambition in 1703 when he was appointed a professor at Oxford, aged forty-seven. From then on he had no more seafaring or spying adventures but it was from this time that he did the astronomical work that most people remember him for.

However, all that time spent at sea had had its effect. Flamsteed grumbled at the change in his friend, saying that Halley 'now talks, swears and drinks brandy like a sea captain'! Well, he *was* a sea captain and he would always love being called 'Captain Halley'.

Predicting the Future

In 1705 Halley published an important book called *A Synopsis of the Astronomy of Comets*. He explained that comets, like planets, are in orbit round the Sun, and are under the influence of Newton's law of gravity just as planets are. By looking back at old records, he had noticed that one comet in particular seemed to come back at regular intervals, roughly every seventy-five or seventy-six years. It had been seen in 1531, 1607 and 1682. Halley realized that it was the same comet going round and round the Sun, not three different comets. Using Newton's law of gravity, he worked out the orbit of the comet and predicted that it would return again in 1758.

When Flamsteed died in 1719 Halley was appointed as the second Astronomer Royal. He carried out many observations, and continued to use the telescopes until a few weeks before he died, on 14 January 1742, aged eighty-five.

On Christmas Day 1758, the comet returned just as he had predicted. It has since been known as Halley's Comet in his honour. This was a scientific sensation at the time because, in a sense, it was the crowning achievement of Newton's work. The scientific laws discovered by people like Newton had all been based on explaining things that had already been observed. It was quite another thing to use the laws to predict something that had *not* yet happened.

Measuring up

Halley's work led to another huge leap in our knowledge of the Universe. In those times people had no idea how big the Universe might be.

As a young astronomer in 1691, Halley had worked out a possible way of measuring the distance from the Earth to the Sun. Some years after his death, his instructions were followed and the measurement from our planet to the Sun was worked out for the very first time. It was found to be equivalent to an amazing 153 million kilometres, a revelation at the time, and very close to the figure we know is the exact one today (149.6 million kilometres).

Halley's great contribution was, like Newton, to prove that the Universe is governed by rules, laws that could be used to predict astronomical events. And he, more than anyone else, helped us get a grip on the sheer size and immensity of the Universe.

All Creatures GREAT and Small

chapter seven

All creatures Great and Small

As the scientific revolution got underway in Europe, people began to investigate everything around them. They weren't just interested in the stars and planets, but in the Earth itself, from the living world of plants, animals and people, to the mystery of when the Earth began . . .

No one had really given the natural world much thought in the seventeenth century. Very little progress had been made since the time of the Greek thinker Aristotle, who had divided animals and plants into a few very basic groups.

Just as the stars and planets had to be counted, listed and measured before people could begin to understand how the heavens worked, so plants and animals had to be identified and catalogued before the living world could be understood. One man started the whole thing off.

John Ray

The son of a humble blacksmith, Ray was the first person to bring some kind of order to the chaotic naming systems that existed for the natural world. It is no surprise that he is often referred to as the father of natural history in Britain.

Ray may have developed his lifelong interest in plants through his mother's knowledge of herbs.

Village life

John Ray was born in the small village of Black

Notley, Essex, in 1627. His father was the village blacksmith and his mother a herbalist and folk healer. She and Ray's father lived a quiet and uneventful life.

Young John was exceptionally bright, and was able to go to school in nearby Braintree where he learnt Latin (but little else). In 1644, at the height of the civil war, he went up to Cambridge, where he also showed a great talent for languages, maths and natural science.

A matter of religion

At that time, Cambridge University was pretty much dominated by the Puritans (very strict Protestants). Ray was sympathetic to their cause but refused to sign an oath declaring his loyalty to them. This was just as well, as in 1660, the king's new rules meant that those who had signed ('Covenanters') were thrown out of their jobs.

A career on hold

After graduating in 1648, Ray stayed on at Cambridge University for the next twelve years, lecturing and also developing a keen interest in botany. As botany was a completely new area of science, there was no one to teach him, so Ray taught himself. With the help of students and friends, he began a major project to list all the plants that grew around Cambridge. One of these friends, wealthy aristocrat Francis Willughby, would become a very significant person in Ray's life. It was with Willughby that Ray went on his first trip to study the plants and animals of Scotland and the north of England.

The English Civil War was also known as the Puritan Revolution. The Puritans and Parliament united against King Charles II, questioning his authority to lay down the law in matters of the Church and the State.

The oath was called a covenant. Those Puritans who signed it were called 'Covenanters'.

In 1660 Ray published his findings in his first book, the Cambridge Catalogue, describing the plants of the area.

A matter of principle

Having avoided the king's wrath so far, in 1662 everything changed for Ray. Charles II decided that everyone in the Church and the universities had to agree to a new law, the Act of Uniformity. This said, among other things, that the Covenanters' oath was now illegal. Even though Ray had never been a Covenanter, he disagreed with the principle and refused to sign the act. For this defiance, he was thrown out of Cambridge.

Friends in high places

With no job to go to, Ray's situation looked desperate. Then in stepped Willughby again. Along with another of Ray's ex-students, the well-off Philip Skippon, they financed a major expedition through Europe to study natural history. Ray would be responsible for plants (Latin name *flora*), Willughby for birds, beasts, insects and fishes (Latin name *fauna*), and Skippon would come along for the ride.

The group travelled through France, Belgium, Holland, Germany, Switzerland, Austria, Italy, Malta and Sicily, making observations and collecting specimens, then returning to England in the year of the Great Fire of London, 1666. Back home, Ray's influential friends continued to help out.

Willughby inherited the grand Middleton Hall, in Warwickshire, a massive place that had plenty of room to house Ray – and all their specimens. Ray became Willughby's private chaplain and set about sorting their vast amount of data and writing up their discoveries.

Willughby and Ray were the first to realize that it was vital to see at first hand the living environment of the plants and animals they were studying. In a way, they were the first ecologists.

Such a lengthy trip was astonishing for those times, and it took years for Ray to organize all their finds.

Death of a Friend

All was well for some years. In 1667 Ray even become a Fellow of the prestigious Royal Society. However, in 1672 Willughby died, leaving Ray an income of £60 a year for life, and a promise that he could stay on at Middleton Hall. But when Willughby's widow, who had never liked Ray, married again, Ray and his wife were forced to move out. They returned to the family home in Black Notley, where they had just enough money to live on while Ray wrote his books.

Ray was also one of the first people to realize that fossils were the remains of living organisms that were now extinct. He called them 'serpent stones'.

In Print at Last

Ray never forgot Willughby's huge kindness to him. When their books were published in later years, Ray refused to take proper credit for all the work he had done, preferring instead to honour his friend. The first book, *Ornithology*, a history of birds, was completed by Ray and published in 1677 in Francis Willughby's name. The second book, *History of Fishes*, also had Willughby's name as author, although it had really been almost entirely written by Ray.

Ray's own book, a huge *History of Plants*, was so big that it was published in three volumes. It was an amazing work that described a staggering 18,000 plants. Ray had single-handedly made the study of the living world a science. He classified everything in orderly and logical ways, and provided the basis for people to begin to understand how the living world worked.

Ray died in 1705. Two years later a boy was born in Sweden who would pick up where Ray left off.

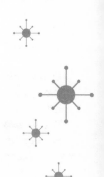

Carl Linnaeus

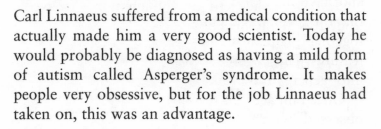

He devoted his life to classifying the natural world and came up with the system we still use today. He also came up with the shocking idea that humans might be related to apes and monkeys . . .

An obsessive nature

Carl Linnaeus suffered from a medical condition that actually made him a very good scientist. Today he would probably be diagnosed as having a mild form of autism called Asperger's syndrome. It makes people very obsessive, but for the job Linnaeus had taken on, this was an advantage.

A helping hand

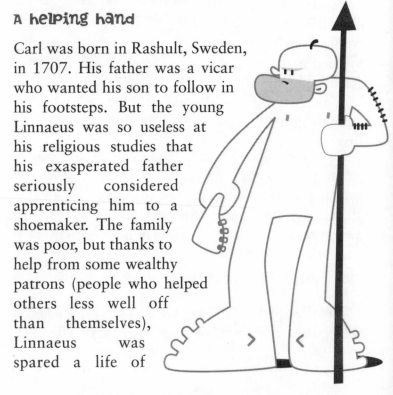

Carl was born in Rashult, Sweden, in 1707. His father was a vicar who wanted his son to follow in his footsteps. But the young Linnaeus was so useless at his religious studies that his exasperated father seriously considered apprenticing him to a shoemaker. The family was poor, but thanks to help from some wealthy patrons (people who helped others less well off than themselves), Linnaeus was spared a life of

Olof Celsius was the uncle of Anders Celsius, who invented the temperature scale we use today. Interestingly, Celsius's original scale started at 100 (freezing) and went down to 0 (boiling)!

shoemaking and sent to university instead, qualifying as a doctor in 1735. One of the people who encouraged him in his studies was the dean of Uppsala Cathedral, Olof Celsius.

putting plants in order

While Linnaeus was studying, he got interested in the new discovery (made in 1717 by the French botanist Sebastian Vaillant) that plants reproduce sexually, and have male and female parts. Linnaeus thought that the plant world could be organized by grouping together plants with the same broad reproductive features. These 'families' could be further subdivided into 'genera' and eventually 'species'.

Once Linnaeus hit on this idea, he became literally obsessed with putting it into action. But this behaviour was just what was needed when it came to classifying thousands of plant species. This task would have bored most people to tears, but Linnaeus loved it and was determined to classify every single plant known in the world.

Linnaeus never quite managed to classify every single one of the world's plants, but he still achieved a phenomenal amount.

Linnaeus also decided that the classification of animals needed his own special attention, and in his first great book, *Systema Naturae*, published in 1735, he covered both plants and animals. He kept on revising and improving the book (another sign of his obsessive nature), and his greatest achievement appeared in the tenth edition, which was published in 1758.

two names for everything

Linnaeus's really clever idea was naming everything consistently according to a logical, orderly system, which could be understood and applied by scientists all over the world. It became known as the binomial

classification, or binomial system, because in it every living species is given a unique two-word name. ('Bi' means 'two', 'nomial' means 'name'.) For example, when biologists refer to the puma or cougar, they call it *Felis concolor*.

Today, the binomial also says something about how animals and plants are related. The first word is the 'genus' – that's the larger group that the subject belongs to. For instance, the puma is in the genus *Felis* (as are other members of the cat family, like the domestic cat). This instantly shows that the puma and the cat are related. The second name combines with the genus name to give the 'species' name. This narrows the classification down to the group of organisms that can breed with each other. Although they are related, cats and pumas are not the same species, as they cannot breed.

Linnaeus also took a very bold step for his time, by including human beings in his classification of animals. People believed that as God had created man in his own image, human beings couldn't possibly be related to animals. Here is the classification for human beings in the modern version of Linnaeus's system:

Linnaeus could have gone further. He once said in a letter that he knew of no real scientific difference between man and ape, but that 'if I call man ape or vice versa, I should bring down all the theologians on my head'.

Kingdom:	Animalia
Phylum:	Chordata
Subphylum:	Vertebrata
Class:	Mammalia
Order:	Primates
Family:	Hominidae
Genus:	Homo
Species:	sapiens

Or, for short, *Homo sapiens*. By putting humans in the order 'Primates', Linnaeus was saying that people are animals and belong to the same wide group as monkeys, chimpanzees and gorillas. This was a daring and shocking idea at the time. Linnaeus would probably not have been able to get away with it if he had lived in Italy, like Galileo.

Linnaeus wasn't afraid to question religious teachings. But he was afraid to say so publicly, in case he got into trouble with the Church. As you'll see later, he would also keep his doubts about the age of the Earth to himself.

A botanical 'anorak'

After qualifying, Linnaeus practised as a doctor for a while, and got married in 1739, eventually having seven children. He was made a professor of medicine at Uppsala University, but swapped to the chair of botany in 1742, a position he held for the rest of his life.

Linnaeus's obsession with order extended to his teaching. He used to take his students out on expeditions that were organized like a military campaign. Everyone had to wear special clothing, jokingly referred to as the 'botanical uniform'. The expedition members always set off at exactly 7 a.m., took a meal break at 2 p.m. and had a short rest at 4 p.m. Professor Linnaeus gave a short talk about the plants they had found precisely every half-hour.

Linnaeus made lists of everything. He could not understand 'anything that is not systematically ordered'. In his lists, Linnaeus was the first person to

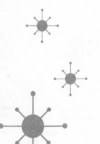

use the astrological symbols for Venus (♀) and Mars (♂) to represent female and male sexes.

This kind of orderliness must have made Linnaeus extremely difficult to live with! His wife certainly seems to have found him exasperating. At home his many collections were banished to an outbuilding on a rocky knoll above his house, which Linnaeus called his 'castle in the air'.

Linnaeus died a revered and respected figure in 1778. He had described, in scientific detail, an astonishing 7,700 species of plants and 4,400 species of animals. His system came just in time to help a whole new group of scientists and explorers. Europeans were exploring the furthest reaches of the Earth and new species were being found all the time. Explorer James Cook would lead the way in mapping the Pacific. A young man who travelled with Cook would really put Linnaeus's new system to the test.

Joseph Banks

An adventurer-cum-naturalist, Joseph Banks accompanied Captain Cook on his first incredible voyage of exploration, bringing back thousands of amazing finds from all over the world.

The gentleman botanist

Joseph Banks was born in London in 1743, the only son of a wealthy landowner. He had a happy childhood roaming wild at the family seat at Revesby, Lincolnshire, and was educated at Harrow, Eton and Christ Church, Oxford.

But despite this impressive education, young

Joseph was no scholar. His Harrow tutor complained that he had an 'immediate love of play', implying that Joseph didn't take his studies seriously enough. However, there was one subject that Joseph did take seriously – plants. He spent all his spare time chatting to local herbalists about the plant world. 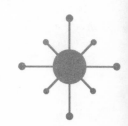 He felt so passionately about the subject that when he went to Oxford and found that the professor of botany there had never given a lecture, he paid Israel Lyons (the most famous botanist of his time) to leave Cambridge and come to Oxford to teach him.

Then, in 1761, tragedy struck when Banks's invalid father died. Joseph wasn't yet twenty-one, so couldn't inherit the family fortune. He left Oxford without taking his degree so he could learn how to run his family's estates. When he finally came of age in 1764, Banks became one of the richest men in England.

The young adventurer

Banks was young, rich and good-looking. He could have simply settled down to a cosseted life of luxury. But there was an unconventional streak in young Joseph. Not for him the staid grand tour of Europe; his grand tour would be nothing short of the entire world!

For starters, he bought himself a ticket on a survey ship, the HMS *Niger*, bound for the remote coastline of Labrador and Newfoundland in

The voyage was an incredible opportunity for Banks. In today's terms, it would be like giving a scientist the chance to journey to and explore another planet.

Canada. When he got back to England, laden with plant specimens and notes, he was elected a Fellow of the Royal Society and bought a smart London residence to house his collections.

secret mission

But that trip was just a taster. He soon heard that the Admiralty and the Royal Society were planning to send a ship, captained by James Cook, to Tahiti, in the South Seas, to make some important observations of the planets.

However, the observations were partly an excuse for some secret exploring, and Cook was given sealed instructions on where to go after Tahiti. The government was keen to extend Britain's influence by discovering new lands, and wanted to discover what riches the Pacific Ocean held. They particularly wanted Cook to find what they believed was a great southern continent in the southern Pacific. Without any real evidence for it, people had believed that a huge, hidden, southern continent must exist to counterbalance the land masses of Europe, Asia and North America. They called it *Terra Australis Incognita*.

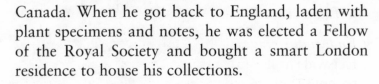

Astronomers had decided that Tahiti was the best place to see an astronomical phenomenon called the transit of Venus. These are very rare events, but in 2004 many people in Britain were lucky enough to see a transit of Venus.

voyage to another world

Thrilled at the prospect of such a voyage, Banks spared no expense. He spent a massive £10,000 (more than £10,000,000 in today's money) on equipment and eight assistants, including two artists and his friend, the botanist Daniel Solander. The great adventure finally got underway when *Endeavour* set sail into the unknown in August 1768.

A tight squeeze

Endeavour was only 107 feet long and less than 30 feet wide at her broadest point. This small space had to house all the ship's stores and ninety-four crew members, not to mention all Banks's scientific equipment and specimens, party of helpers and two greyhounds! Amazingly, despite the horribly cramped conditions, Banks, the rich young gentleman, and Cook, the bluff Yorkshireman, got on incredibly well.

People, plants and stingrays . . .

In 1769, after the observations had been made in Tahiti, *Endeavour* sailed south-west, eventually reaching New Zealand. They were the first Europeans to land here. Banks collected many botanical specimens and wrote the first descriptions to reach Europe of Maori people.

After Cook had mapped the islands of New Zealand, he opened his secret instructions and sailed north-west in search of the Great Southern Continent. Land was sighted again on 17 April 1770. They had reached the east coast of Australia.

At their first landfall, there were so many rays swimming in the waters that Cook decided to call the area Stingray Bay. He changed his mind when he saw the number of specimens Banks collected and called it Botany Bay instead (the name by which it is known today). They continued north, up the coast of the country, which Cook named New South Wales.

An unexpected delay

Cook had to sail through the treacherous Great Barrier Reef, and on 10 June 1770 his worst

Banks wrote the first detailed description of tattooing, an art at which the Maori people excelled.

The dried plant specimens Banks collected on his expeditions are now in the Botany Department of the Natural History Museum in London.

Botany Bay would become infamous as the destination of the first convict settlers. In fact, it was unsuitable for colonization, and they eventually settled further up the coast at Port Jackson, now the vibrant city of Sydney.

nightmare happened – *Endeavour* struck a reef and was holed. Skilfully, the crew managed to 'fother' the hole (plug it with, among other things, a disgusting mixture of wool and animal dung) long enough to sail *Endeavour* into the mouth of a nearby river where they were able to repair her.

This unscheduled six-week stop gave Banks a golden opportunity to explore, observe wildlife and collect even more plants.

A tragic end

Cook eventually realized that there couldn't be a great southern continent of the size that people had thought. After two years at sea, the ship headed for home, stopping off in Java. Tragically, after losing only a handful of men on the hazardous journey so far, almost half of the crew died here of tropical diseases. Both Banks and Solander got severe dysentery, but somehow survived.

One of the saddest losses for Banks was one of his artists Sydney Parkinson, whose wonderfully detailed and accurate drawings set a new standard in natural-history illustration.

A hero's welcome

Endeavour finally arrived back in England in July 1771 to a tremendous welcome, having sailed completely round the world. Cook's reputation was confirmed and he went on to command two more amazing voyages.

His handsome young passenger became a national hero. Banks had brought back hundreds of species of animals and plants from around the world that had never been seen before. He and Solander would spend years classifying them all using Linnaeus's system.

The toast of London society, Banks became a personal friend of the king, George III, was made a baronet in 1781 and helped to establish Kew Gardens as a world-renowned centre of botanical excellence. Banks and his collectors introduced over 7,000 new plant species, many of which are a common sight in gardens today. He was elected President of the Royal Society in 1778, in recognition of his achievements, a post he held until his death in 1820. He was the Society's longest serving president.

Banks was not a great scientist in the mould of Ray or Linnaeus, but he was responsible for ensuring that botany became a popular science and that thousands of new plant species were discovered and classified accurately.

Living plants and animals were not the only things getting a makeover by eighteenth-century scientists – the mysteries of life in the past were also starting to be unravelled.

Banks only travelled abroad once more, to Iceland, but he sent young enthusiastic botanists all over the world to collect plants for the Royal Botanical Gardens at Kew, London.

Banks was always full of bright ideas. It is thanks to him that we all drink Indian tea, as it was he who got the tea plant introduced into India from its native China.

the birth of the earth

the puzzling question of when the earth began caused a clash between the church and men of science. two frenchmen would both work out their own way of estimating its age. but would they let anyone know their results?

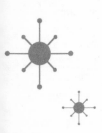

Surprisingly, Ancient Greek and Roman scholars hadn't really thought about the origins of the Earth or how old it might be. Nearly 2,000 years later, by the time of Ray, Linnaeus and Hooke, nothing much had changed. Religious leaders such as Martin Luther had estimated the Earth's age by counting back all the generations in the Bible from Jesus Christ to Adam – Luther came up with an age of 4,000 years old. In 1650, an archbishop named James Ussher went even further – the world was created, he said, at exactly 9 a.m. on Sunday, 26 October 4004 BC, making it roughly 6000 years old. Was this what the Church still agreed with in the eighteenth century?

Some people at the time thought fossils were the remains of creatures drowned in Noah's flood.

Fighting over fossils

By this time, scientists like Linnaeus and Hooke had the idea that fossils were the remains of creatures from a time long, long ago. In his book *Micrographia*, Hooke said that fossils were formed by being filled with mud or petrifying (stone-forming) water, which then hardened over a very long period of time – a pretty accurate description. Neither he nor Linnaeus could see how 6,000 years would be a long enough period of time to create a fossil.

Buffon was so keen to work that he employed a burly servant to drag him out of bed at 5 a.m. each day, and make sure he was awake.

Around the same time that Hooke was writing *Micrographia*, a Danish scientist – known as Steno –

was examining fossilized sharks' teeth, which he had found in rocks a long way from the sea. Aha, said the Church, proof that Noah's flood covered the entire planet with water. Not so, Linnaeus pointed out, taking up Steno's argument. The flood only lasted a matter of months and the amount of sediment required to make these fossil-containing rocks couldn't possibly have been laid down in such a short time.

But Linnaeus never published his ideas, so his doubts about the age of the Earth were not widely known. A rich Frenchman, the Comte de Buffon, however, did.

The comte de Buffon

The man who did the first proper experiment to measure the Earth's age.

Georges-Louis Leclerc, known as the Comte de Buffon, was born in the same year as Linneaus, 1707. His family came into money when Georges was a child and he inherited a fortune from his mother. He was so rich he could have afforded to do nothing for the rest of his life but, like Joseph Banks, he had a passion for science, and turned all his energies to his work.

created by a comet?

Buffon made various scientific achievements in his life, including writing a huge forty-four-volume history of science and being the first person to suggest that coal and oil are the remains of living things. His most intriguing contribution to science, however, was an experiment that sparked off a whole new way of thinking about the Earth's

creation. He had the idea that the Earth might have been formed when a comet passed close to the Sun and pulled out a streamer of hot material from it.

The streamer, thought Buffon, would have formed a molten globe of 'stuff' that would have cooled down and solidified to make the Earth. He then tried to work out accurately how long such a globe would take to cool.

This was really the first scientific attempt to measure the age of the Earth. Buffon's experiment involved heating up balls of iron of different sizes until they were red-hot, then measuring how long it took for them to cool down to the point where they could be held comfortably in the hand.

The Earth gets older

Buffon came up with an age for the Earth of more than 75,000 years, and he wasn't afraid to publish the results of his calculations. To us, this seems small compared with the age of 4.6 *billion* years calculated today, but it was a staggeringly large number for people to try to get their heads round in the eighteenth century.

Revolutionary ideas

The reason why Buffon's number wasn't even larger was realized by another clever Frenchman.

Comets are actually much too small to pull out a streamer of material from the Sun as Buffon suggested, but nobody knew that in the eighteenth century.

One story says that Buffon asked delicate young ladies to help him. Their soft hands, unused to work, made particularly sensitive judges of heat!

In fact, Buffon's wasn't the biggest estimate of the Earth's age. Around 1500, Leonardo da Vinci had estimated some river deposits to be 200,000 years old, and the age of the Earth to be older still.

Jean Fourier

Taking Buffon's ideas a step further, he came up with an even more accurate way of calculating the Earth's age.

Fourier, who was born in 1768, had an eventful life. Indeed, he was lucky to survive the violence of both the French Revolution and the Napoleonic wars. Orphaned when he was only eight years old, he was brought up and educated by monks, eventually becoming a teacher. Some years later he was arrested, for no good reason, during a particularly nasty period of the French Revolution called the Terror (1793–4). He was extremely lucky not to be sent to the guillotine, and after a spell in prison was eventually released.

The French Revolution (1789–99) was essentially a rebellion of the middle classes against the rich and arrogant ruling class. The revolutionaries executed the king and queen and set up a republic.

Fourier went back to teaching and, in an amazing turnaround, became so regarded as a good citizen of revolutionary France, that he was chosen to go with Napoleon on his expedition to conquer Egypt in 1798.

Cooling down period

When he returned to France in 1801, Napoleon gave him an important job in a place called Isère. It was at this time that Fourier investigated how heat is conducted, and while he was doing this he realized that Buffon had made one big mistake in his calculations. He had forgotten that when a really big lump of hot stuff cools down, the outside cools first, and solidifies to make a skin, or crust on the surface. This insulates the hot material inside, slowing down the rate at which heat escapes. So it takes much longer for a lump of red-hot iron as huge as the Earth to cool down than Buffon realized.

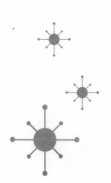

We now call the skin of the Earth its 'crust', and know that it floats on a semi-molten layer in the mantle, the next layer down, between 100 and 660 km below the surface.

A shocking number

But how much longer? This is where Fourier really showed how clever he was. He worked out mathematical laws and equations, which describe how heat flows. These equations, and a technique he developed that is now called Fourier analysis, turned out to be incredibly useful in all kinds of investigations of the world, not just in studying heat.

When Fourier worked out how long it had taken the Earth to cool, he couldn't believe the size of the number. He was so shocked, he never left a record of his result. Instead, he published the formula for everyone to work it out for themselves. Fourier's calculation comes to 100 *million* years. Archbishop Ussher must have been spinning in his grave at the thought!

Fourier died in 1830, from the effects of a disease that he had caught in Egypt. His work in this area was the closest anyone had got to the real age of the Earth at this time.

Even older?

The reason that even this huge number is still so much less than the age we calculate today is because Fourier didn't know anything about radioactivity, which wasn't discovered until nearly the end of the nineteenth century. Radioactivity releases heat deep inside the Earth, and keeps the core hot long after it would otherwise have cooled down.

But as time went on, even before radioactivity was discovered, it became clear 100 million years was still far too short a time to explain origin and evolution of the Earth and life on Earth. But before we get on to that story, let's catch up on what else had been happening in the eighteenth century.

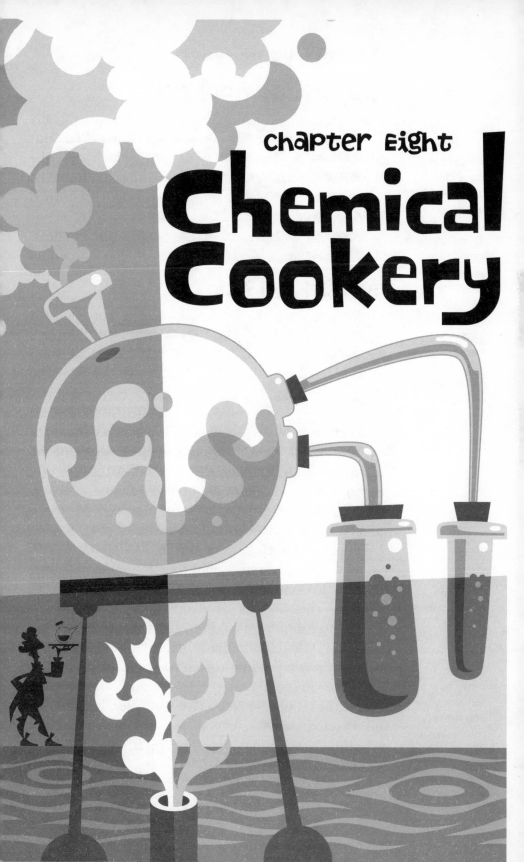

chapter eight

Chemical Cookery

chemical cookery

The late eighteenth century was a time of revolution. The American colonies rebelled against England, and in France the lower classes revolted against their king. Meanwhile, scientists in both countries were having some revolutionary ideas of their own.

joseph black

The man who did more than anyone to turn chemistry into a proper science.

scottish roots

France and Scotland had strong links at that time. France had been Scotland's traditional ally against England – called the 'Auld Alliance' – and there was a lot of trade between the two countries, particularly in Scottish whisky and French wine.

In 1728, a baby boy was born in France to parents of Scottish descent. Young Joseph Black, one of thirteen children, was the son of a prosperous Scottish wine merchant living in Bordeaux.

Joseph's parents were keen for him to know more about his Scottish roots, so he was sent to the University of Glasgow at the age of eighteen. He wanted to study philosophy but his father insisted that he do something more practical. Medicine was just the thing. After studying in Glasgow, Black moved to Edinburgh to do medical research.

All sorts of strange minerals were used as medicines at this time. Unfortunately some, such as mercury, were also highly poisonous – a real case of 'kill or cure'.

During this time, Black tried to find out if a substance called white magnesia could be used as a cure for kidney stones. His careful experiments didn't throw up the results he was after, but had an unexpected pay-off. It was the way Black did his research, and what he discovered, that would transform chemistry.

Made to measure

What made Black stand out from other scientists was that at every stage of his experiments, he weighed everything as accurately as possible. There was absolutely no guesswork involved. Because he did this he discovered that when he heated the magnesia it lost weight. The only explanation he could come up with was that something had escaped from the magnesia into the air. He called that something 'fixed air', because it had been 'fixed' in the white magnesia.

Carbon dioxide (CO_2) didn't get its modern name until later. Carbon dioxide simply means it is made up of one carbon atom to every two oxygen atoms.

The nature of air

Black decided to test his fixed air. As it escaped from the magnesia, he collected some into a glass jar and found that if he put a lighted candle into it the candle went out. Black didn't know it but he had discovered carbon dioxide.

   Black realized that as candles normally stay lit in ordinary air, then air must be a mixture of gases, the fixed air (carbon dioxide) and at least one other gas that *does* allow candles to burn.

A proper science

Black's discoveries made other chemists realize just how important it is to weigh and measure everything accurately. It is this rather nerdy aspect that makes chemistry a proper science, because it measures *quantities*

In Black's time, chemistry was regarded almost as a lowly branch of medicine. Its only purpose was to provide remedies for the treatment of disease.

instead of just describing qualities (such as saying wood burns and stones don't). Science is *quantitative*, not just qualitative.

Black was also interested in heat and was helped in his experiments by a young man named James Watt, who later went on to invent the steam engine. He also had an enormous influence on the teaching of chemistry, being an inspiring teacher – students came from as far away as America to attend Black's lectures. He died in 1799.

Joseph Priestley

A fascinating character of strong political views, he discovered the gas we now know as oxygen, as well as accidentally creating the first fizzy drink.

Son of a weaver

Nonconformists had their own preachers, churches (or chapels) and colleges, which were originally set up to educate young men training to become preachers.

Joseph Priestley had an unsettled early life. He was born the eldest son of a poor weaver, near Leeds, Yorkshire, in 1733. When their tiny cottage became too small to house the growing family (Joseph eventually had five brothers and sisters), Joseph was sent to live with his grandfather, and later his aunt, Sarah.

The Priestley family were members of a religious group called Calvinists. Protestant groups such as the Calvinists and the Puritans were also known as Nonconformists, because they refused to conform to the ways of the official Church of England. It's hard to believe it today, but Nonconformists were not allowed to go to English universities or even have certain jobs.

educating Joseph

Like all Calvinists, Aunt Sarah valued education and made sure that Joseph went to school. He worked hard and the family hoped that he would become a minister, but when he was in his teens he became seriously ill with tuberculosis. His family feared he would die.

Thankfully, Joseph did recover but because of his illness he was nineteen before he could go to an academy to train to become a minister. Here he also learnt history, philosophy and the basics of what we now call science.

After a few years of working as a minister, Priestley discovered he had a real talent for teaching, and in 1761 he started lecturing on classics and history at another Nonconformist academy near Manchester.

Priestley was interested in many subjects – he was outspoken and clever and would go to London for a month every year to meet with the leading thinkers of the London scene and discuss knotty problems of the day, be it politics, religion – or even science.

A fateful meeting

It was on one such visit, in 1765, that Priestley met Benjamin Franklin, the famous American politician and scientist. Priestley was a great supporter of the American colonists, so you can imagine the two men getting on like a house on fire, talking about the latest news from across the Atlantic. Franklin had been working on electricity and infected Priestley with his enthusiasm for the subject. Priestley began to do his own experiments on electricity and his work got him elected a Fellow of the Royal Society. In 1767, Priestley published *The History and Present*

In the days before antibiotics, tuberculosis, or TB, was a common infection, mainly of the lungs. It was also called consumption, as victims seemed to be consumed by the disease.

The education given by the Nonconformist academies was actually better than at Oxford or Cambridge, where you only really learnt anything if, like Newton, you made the effort to study it yourself.

While writing – and making corrections to – his book, Priestley discovered that a strange substance, made from the sap of a South American tree, could be used to rub out pencil marks. He called the substance India rubber – the name stuck!

Priestley never made any money from inventing soda water, but a rich English politician Lord Shelburne heard about it in 1772. He later became Priestley's patron, so even though it didn't make him rich, the invention did help Priestley in his career.

State of Electricity. The same year, Priestley became the minister of a chapel in Leeds, where the nearby brewery stirred his interest in chemistry.

Beer, bubbles and beverages

By this time, scientists knew that the gas that bubbled up out of brewing vats when beer was being made was the 'fixed air' discovered by Joseph Black. This gas formed a layer about 20 cm thick just above the surface of the beer, and Priestley used the brewery as a kind of laboratory to study it. He found that although a burning candle lowered into this layer went out, the smoke from the candle stayed there. He put more smoke into the layer so that he could see how the gas moved, and watched how waves could be made to ripple through it and how the gas flowed over the edge of the vat and down to the floor, suggesting it was heavier than air.

Priestley trapped the gas escaping from the vats and found that he could dissolve it in water. He had invented soda water, the very first fizzy drink. A craze for the new drink soon spread right across Europe.

Becoming a professional scientist

The politician Lord Shelburne was very impressed by Priestley's work and invited him to become Librarian at his country house in Wiltshire. Shelburne was also sympathetic to Priestley's support of the rebellious American colonists.

There wasn't much work to do and Shelburne effectively paid Priestley £250 a year to be on hand to discuss politics, teach Shelburne's two sons, and carry out whatever *chemical* experiments he liked.

priestley's discoveries

Before Priestley began his experiments in Wiltshire, only two gases were known: air itself, and fixed air. In 1776, Henry Cavendish, who we shall meet again shortly, discovered hydrogen, which he called 'inflammable air'. Priestley discovered another ten gases, including ammonia, hydrogen chloride, nitrous oxide, nitrogen dioxide and sulphur dioxide. But his greatest discovery was oxygen.

vital to life

Priestley had discovered that air could be 'used up' so that it would no longer support life. He saw that mice kept in sealed glass containers used up the 'good' air as they breathed, and collapsed when the 'goodness' had gone from it. But they could be revived by putting them in fresh air. He also found that plants could make the air breathable again. This was the first clue to the way plants take carbon dioxide out of the air and release oxygen back into the air: the process that provides all the oxygen we breathe.

On 1 August 1774, Priestley was heating a substance called the red calx of mercury (mercuric oxide). There were no Bunsen burners in those days, so heating things up was difficult. You had to use candles or lamps burning vegetable oil or

Priestley was as radical in his politics as in his religion – he believed in the outrageous idea that ordinary people should elect their government!

Plants make their own food from sunlight, carbon dioxide and water, a process called 'photosynthesis'. Oxygen is a waste product of this process.

spirit, or you could focus the heat of the Sun through a powerful lens. This is what Priestley did.

When the calx was heated it gave off a gas, and turned into pure mercury. Priestley collected the gas and did experiments with it, such as putting a candle into a glass jar full of the 'new' gas. Priestley found that it flared up very brightly. He also found that a mouse could run about happily in a glass box full of this gas for twice as long as in a box the same size full of ordinary air. But although he was an excellent experimenter, Priestley himself never realized exactly what it was that he had discovered and how important it was.

Phlogiston?

In Priestley's day, people believed that when things burnt, something came out of them, because you can see flame and smoke given off by burning things. This 'something' they called 'phlogiston' and they reasoned that the air could absorb phlogiston, like a sponge soaks up water. And, like a sponge soaking up water, air could only absorb a certain amount of phlogiston.

Because things burnt better in the gas he had discovered, Priestley thought it must be air from which all the phlogiston had been taken out, so that it was ready to suck up more. He called it 'dephlogisticated air': what a mouthful!

Not long after making these experiments, Priestley went on a trip to Europe with Lord Shelburne, and in October 1774 they met the leading French chemist, Antoine Lavoisier, in Paris. Priestley told Lavoisier about his discovery.

Lavoisier realized that when things burn they get heavier. That means something is being added, not taken away, so the phlogiston theory couldn't be right. He also realized that the 'something' must come out of the air. It was, of course, oxygen – Priestley's dephlogisticated air. Perhaps Priestley would have worked this out for himself if he had been a full-time scientist. But he was getting more and more involved in politics, and science had to take a back seat.

Moonlit meetings

By 1780, Priestley was becoming so outspoken in his political views that it threatened to harm Shelburne's career, so he agreed to move on, finding a job as a minister in Birmingham.

Birmingham was a boom town in the second half of the eighteenth century, with the Industrial Revolution just getting going. There were lots of people with exciting ideas in science, philosophy, politics and religion in the area, and Priestley became a member of a group who called themselves the Lunar Society.

They got their name because they held their meetings once a month, on the Monday nearest the full Moon, so that it would be bright enough for them to ride home by moonlight afterwards – there were no street lights in the eighteenth century.

The Lunar Society included both of Charles Darwin's grandfathers, Erasmus Darwin and pottery founder Josiah Wedgwood, as well as Priestley's old colleague James Watt.

An angry mob

Priestley's support of the American and French Revolutions got him into real trouble in 1791. One night he and some friends were having dinner when a violent mob, opposed to these revolutionary ideas, rampaged through Birmingham, smashing up Nonconformist chapels and the houses of Priestley's friends. Priestley's house was burnt down, including his library, manuscripts and scientific equipment.

Now nearly sixty, Priestley moved first to London and then, in 1794, emigrated to the new United States of America. He died there in 1804.

Henry cavendish

The other great English chemist of the eighteenth century, cavendish was a strange and obsessively shy character.

The silent scientist

It was said of Cavendish that he probably uttered fewer words in the course of his life than any other man who lived for eighty years.

Henry Cavendish was born in France, like Black. But unlike Black (or Priestley), Cavendish was immensely rich. His parents, Charles and Anne, were aristocrats, and he and his only brother inherited the family's fortune when their father died in 1783.

Cavendish became a talented scientist discovering, among other things, hydrogen gas. But he was incredibly shy, and he didn't tell the world about most of his amazing discoveries. Thankfully he did keep notes of all of his experiments, which were discovered after he died.

Henry was born in Nice, in 1731, where his parents had gone to escape from the English winter, because his mother was suffering from tuberculosis. She died several years later, so Henry and his brother, Frederick, never really had a mother. This may partly explain why Henry grew up to be such a peculiar man.

The boys went to school in London, and then up to Cambridge where, in 1753, poor Frederick fell from an upstairs window. His injuries left him with mild brain damage. He managed a fairly normal life, with the help of servants, but would never study again.

An eccentric life

But Henry was clever enough for both of them. All he was interested in doing was being a scientist, and he set up a laboratory in their London home.

Money meant nothing to Cavendish, despite his wealth. He only ever owned one suit at a time, which he wore every day for years until it was worn out. Then he would buy another suit in exactly the same style, getting more and more old-fashioned as time passed. He must have looked distinctly odd!

Henry also insisted on eating exactly the same thing every day – mutton. Once, when he was expecting some friends for dinner, his housekeeper asked him what to serve. 'A leg of mutton,' he replied. She said this would not be enough. 'Well then,' he said, 'get two.'

social science

Cavendish was painfully shy and only ever went out on scientific business such as Royal Society meetings and dinners – he had become a Fellow in 1760. But even here, if he was late he would wait outside the door until somebody else came along, so that he wouldn't have to go into the room on his own. He communicated with his servants by note, and would hide his face from or run away from women.

When he died in 1810, Cavendish was worth almost exactly one million pounds. This is equivalent to roughly one billion pounds today, making him nearly as rich as Bill Gates, the founder of the Microsoft company.

Home laboratory

*The gas
Cavendish
discovered burnt
so vigorously
that Cavendish
soon decided
that it must be
pure phlogiston
– the substance
people then
believed made
things burn.*

The only things Henry Cavendish spent money on were his laboratories and experiments. He followed Black's example by measuring and weighing everything and was fascinated by gases. He realized that when acid reacts with metal it gives off a gas that is different from both ordinary air and Black's fixed air (carbon dioxide). It burnt very easily, and Cavendish called it 'inflammable air' – today we know it as hydrogen.

Explosive Science

Cavendish was also interested in the way that air seems to be lost when things burn in it. For example, if a candle is burnt in a sealed container with some water in the bottom, the level of water rises as the candle burns. This is because the *volume* of air shrinks – about a fifth of the air disappears before the candle goes out. The reason for this is because one fifth of the air is oxygen, which gets used up in burning.

Although Priestley had already discovered oxygen and found that it makes up about a fifth of ordinary air, Cavendish still tried to explain what was going on in terms of phlogiston. His explanation got horribly complicated but the important thing is that one of the experiments he did while investigating all this involved exploding oxygen (dephlogisticated air) and hydrogen (phlogiston) together in a metal container, using an electric spark.

water on the brain

Apart from making a satisfying bang, the experiment created water – in the explosion the hydrogen and oxygen combined to make H_2O! Cavendish found that his two gases always joined together in the same proportions, two to one, to make water. He weighed everything carefully before and after each experiment, so he found that the weight of water produced was exactly the same as the weight of gas lost.

This was a key moment in chemistry because it showed that water is a *compound*. It is made by two other substances joining together, always in the same proportions – two to one, exactly.

This was the first step towards understanding how atoms combine to make molecules. Cavendish couldn't make this mental leap, because he was still stuck on the idea of phlogiston.

strangely resistant

As well as chemistry, Cavendish also made discoveries in physics. You may have grappled with Ohm's law in physics lessons. Well, don't blame Ohm, Cavendish actually discovered this law years before but never published it.

He lived to a ripe old age for those times, dying quietly at home in 1810, aged seventy-eight – sixteen years after the much less natural death in France of the man who would develop his ideas further, Antoine Lavoisier.

A tribute to Cavendish described him as 'the richest of the wise, and the wisest of the rich'.

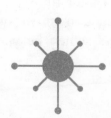

Antoine Lavoisier

Lavoisier wrote a scientific paper about the mineral gypsum, which was used to make the plaster on the walls of houses in Paris. It became known as 'plaster of Paris' as a result.

One of France's greatest scientists, the terrors of the French Revolution would bring about an untimely end to his life.

French Chemistry

Born in 1743, Antoine Lavoisier was only five when his mother died leaving him to be brought up by his Aunt Marie. In 1761 he began studying law at the University of Paris, qualifying as a lawyer in 1764. He also studied astronomy, mathematics, botany, geology and chemistry, all of which he found a lot more interesting than dry and dusty old law.

Although he could have made a good living as a lawyer, Antoine decided to be a scientist instead and he spent the next three years helping Jean-Etienne Guettard to make a geological map of France.

Scientific accolade

In 1766 Lavoisier's grandmother died, leaving him enough money to live on for the rest of his life – he could devote all his time to science. Antoine was fascinated by the discoveries in chemistry going on in England. He studied Black's fixed air and the properties of Priestley's fizzy mineral water. But in 1767 he dropped his chemical experiments, and turned his attention to electricity.

He did rather well, winning a gold medal from the French Royal Academy of Sciences for an essay he wrote on how to light the streets of Paris at night, and being elected a member of the French Royal Academy in 1768, when he was still only twenty-five.

An unpopular job

Although Lavoisier had enough money to live on, when he got an opportunity to increase his income by becoming, in effect, a tax collector, he leapt at the chance. France had a strange and unfair tax system. The king granted licences to various rich gentlemen, known as fermiers, to collect taxes – the more taxes they collected, the more money they made. Hardly surprisingly, the ordinary people hated the system.

The fermiers didn't collect the tax themselves but employed others, often unsavoury characters, to do the dirty work.

Arranged marriage

In 1771, when he was twenty-eight, Lavoisier married Marie-Anne-Pierrette Paulze, the beautiful thirteen-year-old daughter of one of his fellow fermiers. Although the marriage was an arranged one, the couple were very happy together and Marie helped Antoine in many of his experiments. She would probably have been a good scientist in her own right if women had been allowed to do science properly in those days.

Lavoisier used a huge lens, 120 cm across and 15 cm thick to concentrate the heat of the Sun for his experiments.

Chemical discoveries

Like Black, Lavoisier realized that when things burn they get heavier. He also found that when metals burn air to create a substance called a calx, something from the air combines with them. Lavoisier met

Priestley when he visited Paris in 1774, and Lavoisier reckoned that the 'something' was Priestley's dephlogisticated air. He was right; dephlogisticated air, remember, is oxygen, and a calx was what we would call an oxide.

The first 'guinea pigs'

Lavoisier made some interesting discoveries about the process of respiration, which he realized is rather like burning. When something is burnt in air, it makes fixed air (carbon dioxide) and gives off heat; animals also produce carbon dioxide and heat, through respiration.

He tested his idea on guinea pigs, helped by another scientist Pierre Laplace (1749–1827) and Marie.

They put a guinea pig in a container surrounded by ice. After ten hours, the warmth of the guinea pig's body had melted thirteen ounces of ice. Then they burnt small pieces of charcoal in the same sort of container to find out how much needed to be burnt to *also* melt thirteen ounces of ice. They then measured how much fixed air the guinea pig breathed out in ten hours while it was resting, and how much fixed air the charcoal gave off while it was burning. They found that the two

Some people think that it is thanks to Lavoisier's experiments with real guinea pigs that people who volunteer to have experiments carried out on them are often called 'guinea pigs'.

Elements are substances that cannot be broken down into anything simpler by chemical processes but can combine with one another to make more complicated things (like water and carbon dioxide).

amounts were the same. This meant, said Lavoisier, that respiration and burning must generate heat in exactly the same way.

Farewell Phlogiston

Lavoisier was convinced that the old phlogiston theory was dead in the water. He also realized that Cavendish's experiments exploding hydrogen and oxygen together proved that water is a combination of these two gases, and figured that carbon dioxide is a combination of carbon and oxygen. He got rid of the old Greek idea of everything being made of earth, air, fire and water, and gave scientific names to elements such as carbon, hydrogen and oxygen. He set up a logical system for naming chemical substances, just as Linnaeus set up a logical method for naming living things.

In 1789 he published his life's work in *Traité Elementaire de Chimie* (*Elements of Chemistry*). This book really marks the beginning of modern chemistry. But it was published only just in time. Within a year, his decision to become a fermier would cost him his life.

A Violent End

At first Lavoisier thought that France's revolution was a good thing – the corrupt French political system desperately needed reform. But after a few years, what had started out as reform turned into bloody revolution. The king and many members of the ruling class were executed. And the victims included the hated fermiers. Even though Lavoisier wanted reform, this counted for nothing and on 8 May 1794 he was executed at the guillotine. France had lost one of its greatest scientists.

Lavoisier served the new French government well, even working on the committee that later introduced the metric system of weights and measures.

Antoine's wife, Marie, however, survived and would become involved with another great scientist whose own life had been transformed by rebellion on the other side of the Atlantic. His special interest was heat, and his story belongs in the next chapter.

CHAPTER NINE

Turning Up...

the Heat

Turning up the Heat

In the eighteenth and nineteenth centuries, one of the hottest topics in science was heat itself. Heat was crucial to the Industrial Revolution because it could not have happened without the invention of the steam engine.

Different types of heat

As we have already seen, Joseph Black was a mover and shaker in the world of chemistry – but he also created a stir with his heat experiments.

Black was fascinated by the fact that even though ice absorbs a lot of heat while it is melting, its temperature stays at 0°C. In the same sort of way, when water vapour condenses to make steam it gives out lots of heat but its temperature stays the same too, at 100°C.

Black realized there were two types of heat – he called the heat that a solid absorbs while melting, or that a vapour gives out while condensing, without any change in temperature, 'latent heat'. 'Specific heat' was the amount of heat needed to increase the temperature of a certain quantity of a substance by a certain temperature (for instance, the amount of heat needed to increase the temperature of one gram of water by one degree Celsius).

Black carried out lots of experiments with water, ice and steam, helped by a young instrument-maker at the University of Glasgow named James Watt. All this came in very useful for Watt when he got interested in steam engines himself.

James Watt

His idea for an efficient steam engine transformed industry and led to fame and fortune.

As a child, James entertained himself by taking toys apart and making new ones out of all the bits – very useful skills for his future career.

James Watt came from Greenock in Scotland. He was eight years younger than Black, being born on 19 January 1736. He suffered badly from asthma and bronchitis as a young child and couldn't go to school. His mother taught him at home instead and eventually he was able to attend the local grammar school.

James's lack of education didn't seem to matter, because he was always much happier making models and tinkering with machinery in his shipbuilder father's workshop – a sign of his future skill in engineering. But, years later, when his father's business started to fail, James had to find a way to make a living. Because there would be little for him to inherit, he was sent to London to learn a trade at the age of nineteen. He paid twenty guineas – a small fortune then – to be taught instrument-making by one of the top makers in the country. When he returned to Scotland in 1756, he got a job at Glasgow University and met Black.

Hit or myth

There is a famous story about how James Watt is supposed to have got his great idea about powering engines with steam while watching his aunt's kettle boil. Young James, says the tale, realized the power of steam when he saw the lid of a boiling kettle being lifted up by the pressure of the steam underneath. This isn't strictly true. What James discovered was

Thomas Newcomen invented his type of steam engine to pump water out of mines to stop them flooding. The first one was installed in a coal mine in Dudley Castle, Staffordshire, in 1712.

Newcomen engines were also called 'atmospheric engines' because of this effect.

much more subtle, and clever. What fascinated him was the way the steam from his aunt's kettle settled into water droplets when he held a cold cup or a cold metal spoon in the steam jet. He would remember this image of steam condensing on a cold surface years later when he was asked to solve the puzzle of why a model of a pumping engine wouldn't work.

From condensation to inspiration

In 1763, Watt was asked to repair the university's working model of a Newcomen steam engine. Newcomen engines were massive machines consisting of a boiler attached to a cylinder with a piston inside. Above this was mounted a long beam – like a see-saw – attached to a weight at one end and the top of the piston at the other. When the weight pulled down one end of the beam, the other end pulled the piston up. The cylinder then filled with steam from the boiler and a jet of cold water that was sprayed into the cylinder rapidly cooled and condensed the steam. This created a vacuum in the cylinder and the weight of atmospheric pressure pushed the piston down.

This cycle was repeated over and over creating an up-and-down motion. However, the big problem was that the cooling jet of water also cooled down the cylinder, which then had to be completely reheated, making the whole process very slow.

Watt realized this was a very inefficient use of energy. He understood from his work with Black that the metal cylinder had a large specific heat. This led Watt to the bright idea of using two cylinders, one which was kept hot all the time, with the piston moving up and down in it, and the other kept cold all the time, where the steam condensed. This new design worked brilliantly and was nearly seventy-five per cent more efficient.

The important thing about Watt's engine was the separate condenser. But he also had the idea of letting hot steam go into the top of the hot cylinder under pressure, so that it pushed the piston down harder than the weight of the atmosphere could. That is why it is called a steam engine rather than an atmospheric engine, and why Watt is credited with its invention.

Going into business

Although Watt's improvement of the steam engine was a great idea, it didn't make him a rich man straight away. Most mines carried on using the old Newcomen engines that they were used to. Watt moved on. He did a short stint as a surveyor on the Scottish canals but when his wife died in 1773, he moved to Birmingham. Here he joined the Lunar Society, and eventually went into partnership with one of the other members, Matthew Boulton. Together they developed the steam engine commercially.

Watt had his idea of condensing steam in a separate vessel while wandering around Glasgow one day. His inspiration really sparked off the Industrial Revolution and a memorial now marks the very spot.

The Boulton–Watt partnership was hugely successful. Steam engines came to be widely used, and both partners got rich. Steam became the power behind the Industrial Revolution; Boulton and Watt engines powered textile mills, factories and mines.

But although Watt lived until 1819, and made many improvements to his engines, it was left to Richard Trevithick (1771–1833) to take the step of developing small, high-pressure steam engines that could propel themselves along roads and railways. In 1804, he built the world's first railway locomotive.

By the beginning of the nineteenth century, scientists were at last beginning to understand what heat was all about. One huge step forward was taken by one of the most colourful scientists who ever lived.

In 1882, the British Association named the unit of electrical power a watt – so James Watt's name is still written on every light bulb.

Benjamin Thompson

A clever and ambitious man, he made a big leap forward in our understanding of energy. As well as being a scientist, he was also a soldier, statesman, spy and inventor.

Born plain old Benjamin Thompson, in Woburn, Massachusetts, in 1753, this colourful character would die as the much more glamorous Count Rumford, in Paris, in 1814.

Thompson was entirely self-taught. He was fascinated in science from an early age, being interested in eclipses and perpetual motion machines.

At the time Benjamin Thompson was born, Massachusetts was still a British colony. He came from a poor farming family, with many younger brothers and sisters, and had no hope of anything except a basic education, because he had to work to help support them.

Although he didn't have a formal education, he became a teacher in Rumford, Massachusetts, where he soon married a wealthy thirty-year-old widow in 1772, when he was just nineteen.

American rebellion

Now he didn't have to work for a living, Thompson might have settled down to a quiet life. But he was soon swept up in the political turmoil of the times.

Everybody knew that trouble was brewing between the ruling British and the American colonists who wanted more independence. Now he was a landowning gentleman, Thompson decided he was in favour of the way things were. He regarded himself as a loyalist and even worked as a spy for the British. But when the rebellion in America was successful, he had to leave for England and start a new life, leaving his wife and daughter behind.

tinker, tailor, soldier, spy

Thompson was charming and ambitious and had a knack of being in the right place at the right time. In some respects, he was a kind of confidence trickster, talking his way into getting the work he wanted. He managed to get himself all sorts of different jobs in England and Europe, including being an assistant to the secretary of state for the colonies and a military aide to Elector Carl Theodor of Hanover (the ruler of Bavaria, part of present-day Germany).

For this latest job, Thompson needed a title to satisfy the snobby members of the elector's court. In 1784, Thompson went back to London and asked King George III for a knighthood. In return, he offered to spy on the Bavarians for the British. Amazingly, the king agreed. Thomson got his knighthood and the British ambassador in Vienna began to get excellent service from his new spy in Munich, *Sir* Benjamin Thompson.

scientific applications

During all this time, Thompson was developing his interests in science. In England, he did experiments to improve the explosive power of gunpowder. This work was so impressive that in 1779 it got him elected as a Fellow of the Royal Society.

In Bavaria, he soon became the elector's right-hand man, the second most powerful person in the country. He reorganized the army and made it more efficient without spending any extra money. The soldiers' conditions and health improved vastly and morale became much better.

the inventor

Thompson was an inventive man who had lots of ideas for useful things. He developed the first closed kitchen ranges, a bit like Aga cookers, to replace smoky indoor cooking fires. He invented a portable stove for the army to use when it was not in barracks, and an efficient coffee percolator. As his success grew, the elector gave him more and more work, until he became (all at the same time!) Minister of War, Minister of Police, State Councillor and Chamberlain to the Court, with the military rank of Major General!

from countryman to count

In 1792 came the icing on the cake. The Holy Roman Emperor died, and Carl Theodor took over until a new, permanent emperor could be elected. He was in power for just long enough to hand out some titles to his favourites. So Major-General Sir Benjamin Thompson became a count. He chose Count Rumford for his title, in recognition of the town where he had first made his fortune. We'll continue to call him Thompson, though, to avoid confusion.

on his travels

By 1792, Thompson was getting worn out by all the work he was doing in Bavaria. War was brewing in Europe and he got permission to go first to Italy, then England. He stayed in London for nearly a year, revelling in his status as a wealthy nobleman and scientist.

In 1797, Thompson finally returned to Bavaria fired with scientific enthusiasm from his time in Europe, and it was at this time that he did his most important scientific work.

While in England, Thompson designed an efficient kind of chimney, still used today, to stop smoke from open fires billowing out into a room.

In the firing line

It was the discovery he made when put in charge of making new cannon at the Munich Arsenal that was so significant. At this time people thought heat was caused by a kind of fluid, which they called 'caloric'. They said that if two things were rubbed together they got hot because caloric was being squeezed out of them, like water being squeezed out of a sponge.

Cannon were made by grinding a hole through the centre of a solid metal cylinder with a sharp drill. Horse power was used to rotate the cylinder against the drill bit. In the process of grinding, everything got very hot. Thompson was impressed not only by how much heat was produced by the cannon-boring but also by the way the heat kept on being generated. As long as the boring was going on, the cannon got hot. If escaping caloric caused heat, he reasoned, it should all get used up eventually, like all the water being squeezed out of a sponge to leave it dry.

The words 'calorie' – the amount of heat needed to raise one gram of a substance by 1°C – and 'caloric' both come from the Latin calor, *meaning heat.*

To prove his theory, he cleverly found a way to measure how much heat was being generated. He got some spare lumps of metal and sealed them in a box full of water while

The Royal Institution became a huge success, and is still going today. It is particularly famous for its Christmas lectures for children, which are broadcast on TV each year.

they were being ground. The water got hot very quickly, soon coming to the boil. Once the water boiled, Thompson threw it away and started again. It always took the same time to boil the same amount of water, and there was no sign of caloric being used up.

Heat and motion

Thompson thought that heat must be connected to motion in some way, and he was the first person to make this important scientific connection. Nobody would really be able to understand what *kind* of motion until scientists understood more about the way atoms behave, how they stick together to make molecules and how they move. But Thompson himself realized that heat has something to do with work, and that (in modern terms) it is a form of energy that gets passed on from one place to another.

The nature of energy

Thompson realized that his method of boiling water was not very useful, because it depended on the work being done by the horses. The horses that turned the metal cylinder had to be fed, and used some of the energy in their food to keep themselves warm. If you just wanted to boil water, he pointed out, it would be much more efficient to burn the straw they ate in a fire and heat the water directly. He was getting to the important idea that energy cannot be destroyed, only passed on to a different level. The person who finally realized what this really meant was a German doctor called Julius von Mayer. We'll come to him later.

The Royal Institution

In 1798, Thompson returned to London. There, he got together with Joseph Banks to set up a new kind of scientific centre, which eventually became the Royal Institution. This was partly a museum, partly a laboratory where scientists could do research, but most of all it was a place where scientists could give public lectures and describe their work to ordinary people.

Thompson didn't stay in England for long. In 1801 he went back to Europe, and in Paris his life took another twist – he met Marie Lavoisier, the widow of Antoine Lavoisier, and they fell in love. They set up home together in Paris, marrying in 1805 (Thompson's first wife had died several years before). Thompson eventually died in Paris in 1814.

Julius von Mayer

A voyage to a warmer climate sparked off Mayer's ideas about energy, which took Thompson's work to the next level.

It's in the blood

Born in 1814, the year Thompson died, Julius von Mayer trained as a doctor and, in 1840, found himself a job as the physician on a Dutch ship bound for the East Indies. In those days, when people got ill doctors often used to make a small nick in one of their veins to let out a little blood, just as they had back in the Middle Ages.

'Bleeding' or 'bloodletting' was used as a cure for all sorts of ailments right up until the late nineteenth century when it was finally realized that it did no good at all.

From Lavoisier's discovery, Mayer knew that respiration is a form of slow combustion.

Mayer was used to seeing the difference between dark blood from the veins (which doesn't have much oxygen in it) and bright scarlet blood from the arteries (which is packed with oxygen). So he was amazed when he opened the vein of a sailor when the ship was in Java, in the hot East Indies, and saw bright scarlet blood flow out. At first, he thought he had nicked an artery by mistake. But he hadn't.

Mayer checked the blood of some of the other sailors, and even his own, and found exactly the same thing. He realized that the blood in their veins must be red because it still had lots of oxygen in it. Their bodies had used up less oxygen in respiration because it was easy for the sailors to keep warm in the tropical heat. This could only mean one thing: that all kinds of heat energy are really the same thing. It didn't matter whether the body got its warmth from respiration or from the Sun, as long as it was warm.

Mayer's discovery sounds obvious to us. But it was a huge step forward to understand that energy is never actually created or destroyed – it is just changed from one form to another. This was what Thompson had half-realized with his horses, and the chain of energy that started with them eating straw and ended with cannon barrels getting hot.

When Mayer got back to Germany at the end of the voyage, he wrote various scientific papers about his discoveries but nobody took any notice. Eventually other people started to make the same discoveries and got a lot of attention for their work. Mayer got so depressed that, in 1850, he tried to kill himself. But, fortunately, he recovered, and before he died in 1878 he finally got the recognition he deserved.

Heat theory

By the time Mayer died, the last pieces in the jigsaw puzzle of the nature of heat had been slotted into place. Several scientists contributed to these discoveries, including Sadi Carnot (1796–1832), Rudolf Clausius (1822–1888), James Joule (1818–1889), James Clerk Maxwell (1831–1879) and Ludwig Boltzmann (1844–1906). There is no room to tell all their stories here but we can tell you what they discovered. It is called the kinetic theory.

The kinetic theory explains, among other things, the differences between solids, liquids and gases, and the nature of latent heat. In a solid, the atoms and molecules stick together side by side so that they cannot move about, except for a kind of jiggling on the spot. When the solid gets warmer, the atoms and molecules jiggle about more and more. At melting point, they begin to slide past one another.

In a liquid, the particles already slide past each other more easily, and as it gets hotter and they move faster – that is, as a particle gets hotter – it has more kinetic energy. But the particles still have 'stickiness' to each other.

At boiling point, particles begin to move so fast that they get completely unstuck, escape from the liquid and fly off into the air, or into space. In a gas,

'Kinetic' comes from the Greek word for movement, kinētikos, because it is all about the way atoms and molecules move.

The latent heat of a solid is the energy needed to make all of the particles come unstuck from their positions and start to slide past one another. At this point, the material changes from a solid to a liquid.

Air molecules move at about 500 metres per second. There are so many of them that each one has about four billion collisions every second. These collisions against your skin make the air feel like a smooth fluid.

the atoms and molecules fly about so fast that they don't notice the stickiness of their neighbours. They behave just like little hard billiard balls, bouncing off each other and anything they hit, such as your skin or the walls of a container.

So Benjamin Thompson was right when he said that heat is a form of motion. The hotter something gets, the faster the atoms and molecules in it are moving. In a solid, they are jiggling about in one place, in a liquid they are sliding past one another, and in a gas they are whizzing about and bouncing off one another. We'll explain how people got to know that everything is made of atoms and molecules later. Now, though, we want to get back to the story of fossils and how their discovery revealed the ancient history of our planet.

chapter ten

Digging for Dinosaurs

Digging for Dinosaurs

> At the beginning of the nineteenth century no one had any idea that giant reptiles once roamed the Earth. By the end of the century the word 'dinosaur' had become a household name.

William Smith

> The man who put fossils in their place.

Fascinated by Fossils

William Smith was born in the Oxfordshire village of Churchill in 1769, the son of the village blacksmith. Sadly, William's father died when he was only eight and he was largely brought up by his farming uncle and aunt.

It was on his uncle's farm that the young William first became interested in fossils. The fields in his part of Oxfordshire were littered with many strange stones – all were more or less circular, about ten centimetres across, with a rounded top and faint markings. Each stone weighed roughly twenty-two ounces (600 grams).

William and his friends played a game, rather like marbles, with smaller acorn-shaped fossils that they often found in their area.

William was fascinated and puzzled by the stones. Where had they come from and why were they so similar? (He didn't know it but they were actually the fossilized remains of sea urchins.) A lifelong interest in fossils had been sparked off.

A timely career

Although William was clever – he did really well at school – there was no hope of him going to university, as it was simply too expensive. So instead, he taught himself as much as he could from books and became interested in surveying.

This was a really good choice of career. The Industrial Revolution was in full swing in England at the time. New roads and canals were being built all over the country, common land was being enclosed and fenced off to make large farms, and the rich gentlemen of England were paying good money to have their country estates redesigned. All this activity provided plenty of work for surveyors.

William's first job was as an assistant surveyor to Edward Webb. He and Webb travelled widely, which meant that Smith was able to see at first hand the different kinds of landscape and rocks around the country.

Surveyors measure landscape features such as hills and valleys, also buildings and distances, and plot where roads, canals and other structures are going to be built.

A mine of information

In 1791, Smith got a job with a coal-mining company in Somerset. This gave him a fantastic opportunity to go deep down into the mineshafts to study the different layers of rock – called strata – below the surface.

Smith noticed that the strata were very distinct. One layer changed to another very sharply. There might be sandstone in one layer then limestone beneath it, each with a distinct edge. The layers of rock always came in the same order, with coal

Smith also noticed that deeper down the mines the strata seemed to have been bent and squeezed, as if crushed in a giant hand.

The science of studying the sequence of rocks of an area is called 'stratigraphy', from the word 'stratum'.

always in the same places in the sequence, and the rock layers were all of the same thickness.

His first big discovery

At first glance, the many different layers of limestone, sandstone and coal in the rock sequence looked exactly the same. But then Smith realized that each layer of rock contained its own particular set of fossils, and that the fossils always appeared in the same order going up through the strata. This meant he could identify the exact layer of rock in the sequence he was dealing with simply by looking at the fossils it contained. Just by standing in a field and picking up a few stones he could say which rock layer was directly beneath the soil. Because he knew the sequence, once he had identified the top layer of rock, he could predict what strata lay lower down beneath his feet, even without digging a shaft. Most importantly, because he knew where the coal seams were in the sequence of rocks, he could also tell where coal would be found, and how deep it would be, without moving from one place. This was incredibly useful to the mining company.

Smith then began to wonder if all the rocks of Britain were arranged in a similar orderly fashion. He longed to find out, and became so obsessed with studying strata that he got the nickname 'Strata Smith'.

Canal building reached a peak in the 1830s when Britain was criss-crossed by a network of waterways. In 1840 there were nearly 4,500 miles of canals.

Canal cutting

His chance came along soon enough. The coal mined in Somerset had to be transported to where it was needed and in the 1790s, the obvious way to do this was by canal – a much faster alternative to horse-drawn carriages and pack mules.

The obvious person to take charge of building the canal was, of course, Smith. William was delighted. Not only was this a really good job but it also involved making cuttings through hills so that he would be able to see the rock strata. On a six-week research trip, he saw exposed strata in fresh canal cuttings all over England – he was now becoming so knowledgeable about rocks that he could read the strata like the pages of a book.

Smith's hard work was really paying off. He was now earning more than £400 a year and had made enough of a name for himself to become a member of the Royal Bath and West of England Society, a kind of gentlemen's club that included rich landowners, eminent fossil collectors and men interested in new methods of agriculture.

A cunning plan

The agricultural enthusiasts were very good at making plans that showed the features of their land. This gave Smith the idea of making geological maps, coloured to show the strata that lay beneath the surface. He had the grand idea of making a geological map of Britain, or at least of England. As a first step, in 1799 he made a geological map (the first one ever made) of the region round Bath, covering a circle of just ten miles across.

Sacked!

Despite his hard work, in 1799 Smith was sacked from the Somerset Coal Canal Company. The reason is lost in the mists of time but perhaps he was spending too much time on his maps rather than doing his job!

In fact, it suited Smith to work as a freelance

In 1803, the president of the Royal Society, Sir Joseph Banks, heard about the project, and not only encouraged Smith to persevere but gave him £50 to help with his expenses.

In spite of his troubles, Smith's great map was eventually finished, and published in 1815, the year Napoleon was finally defeated at Waterloo. This marked the end of the Napoleonic Wars.

surveyor, because he could fit in his map-making as well. The more he travelled for his work, the more he learnt for his map-making.

Money problems

In order to impress his customers, Smith always bought or rented grander offices and houses than were really necessary. Image and status were everything in those days. However, within a few years, Smith began to run into serious financial trouble.

Imprisoned

By 1815 the long years of war with France were finally over. But the country had to face up to the enormous cost of the war. Rich men cut back spending on their estates and there was high unemployment. Smith found himself out of work and got more and more into debt. Eventually, in 1819, he was sent to prison because he couldn't pay up.

The idea of a debtors' prison is strange to us, because if somebody is in prison there is no chance that they can earn money to pay off their debts. But in the nineteenth century debtors had to rely on friends or patrons bailing them out. Thankfully, Smith was only in prison for two months because all his property was sold off by the bailiffs to pay his debts. He was released in August 1819, when he was fifty years old – free but penniless.

A new start

Things were so bad that they

could only get better. With his wife and his orphaned, eighteen-year-old nephew, John Phillips, Smith set off for Yorkshire. Here he lived as a freelance surveyor until he died, aged seventy, in 1839. By then his achievements had been properly recognized, and he had many honours heaped upon him. Smith's work was so important that he has been called the father of English geology.

Geology is the scientific study of the origin, history and structure of the Earth.

The importance of geology

The things Smith discovered in geology didn't just tell people how to do useful tasks like finding coal seams. They also led to a deeper understanding of the nature of life and, eventually, evolution.

Rocks are formed in many different ways. Sedimentary rocks, for instance, such as sandstone or limestone, are formed when mud, sand or other sediments collect at the bottom of the sea or a lake, and get squashed over millions of years as more and more sediment is laid down on top of them. Another type of rock – igneous rock – is formed when lava pours out of volcanoes and solidifies. Where rocks are laid down in layers, one on top of the other, it's pretty obvious that the deeper strata were laid down before the top ones – the youngest strata are at the top, and the oldest strata are at the bottom.

Many sorts of sedimentary rocks have fossils in them – the remains of animals and plants that lived when the original sediments were laid down. The different fossils found in the strata – from the deepest layers right up to the surface – reflect the changes in the environment, and the animals and plants that lived there over thousands or millions of

Scientists have only been able to give actual ages to rocks since the mid twentieth century, by measuring tiny amounts of natural radioactivity in them. This is called 'radiometric dating'.

Geologists who study fossils and past environments are known as 'palaeontologists'.

years. Fossils have shown that past environments and life forms on Earth were sometimes very different from those we know today. They also showed that the age of the Earth was far longer than Archbishop Ussher's paltry 6,000 years.

Georges Cuvier

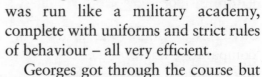

People were amazed at the incredible creatures he reconstructed from fossil remains.

The French Fossil hunter

Georges Cuvier was born in the same year as William Smith, 1769, in a city called Montbéliard, on the border between France and Switzerland.

Cuvier's father wasn't rich but Georges was his favourite son and he always got the best the family could provide. He went to school and, thanks to some connections of his father's, he managed to get a free place at the new University of Stuttgart when he was only fifteen.

Cuvier was really interested in natural history. He had read Buffon's *Histoire Naturelle* from cover to cover when he was just a boy but there was nothing interesting like this being taught at Stuttgart. The place

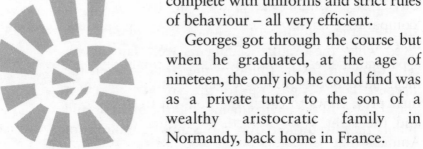

was run like a military academy, complete with uniforms and strict rules of behaviour – all very efficient.

Georges got through the course but when he graduated, at the age of nineteen, the only job he could find was as a private tutor to the son of a wealthy aristocratic family in Normandy, back home in France.

Escaping the terror

With the French Revolution looming, this was a bad time to be associated with an aristocrat. Remember the revolutionaries hated the wealthy classes? But luckily for Cuvier, it took a while for the revolution to reach Normandy, and for the next few years he was able to live quietly in the countryside, untouched by its horrors. He became interested in botany, and decided to follow the example of Linnaeus and Ray by identifying and classifying many species of plants. He published his work and exchanged letters with other botanists all over Europe. But, in 1793, Louis XVI and his queen, Marie Antoinette, were executed, and the reign of terror began. Cuvier's quiet scientific life was shattered.

Cuvier had supported the revolution in the beginnings but, like many others, the violence of the Terror sickened him.

For more than a year, France went mad. Thousands of people were sent to the guillotine. Thankfully, Cuvier was saved by his common sense. Despite his growing concern at the behaviour of the revolutionaries, he decided to become an official for the revolutionary government. Then, in 1795, when life in France was beginning to return to normal, Cuvier, now twenty-six, combined his scientific skills and his experience as an administrator to get a job at the Museum of Natural History in Paris. He stayed there for the rest of his life.

Cuvier's work

Cuvier was highly regarded for his work in 'comparative anatomy' – a way of studying animals that explained how their bodies work to fit them for a particular lifestyle. For example, animals that eat meat have bodies suited for fast running to catch their prey, claws to catch and hold on to their prey, and the right kind of teeth for biting into flesh. Animals that eat plants might also have to run fast

In 1831 Cuvier was made a baron, which was a very rare honour for a Protestant in France in those days.

Cuvier named pterodactyl from the Greek words pteron *and* daktulos, *meaning 'winged finger'.*

but they don't need claws, so they can have hooves, which will give them a better grip on the ground. They don't have cutting teeth but big flat teeth for grinding up plants.

Cuvier boasted that an expert (he meant himself!) could reconstruct an entire animal from a single bone. This was an exaggeration but it is true that identifying a single tooth can tell you whether the animal it came from was a meat-eater with claws or a plant-eater with hooves, even if you have never seen the animal.

This is what made Cuvier's work so important. Because he understood how animals work, he could reconstruct animals that had never been seen by anybody, from bits and pieces of their fossil remains. One of the animals he reconstructed in this way was the flying dinosaur, pterodactyl.

Life on Earth

Cuvier identified which fossils occur in which strata in the rocks around Paris. Like Smith, he learnt to put them in the correct order through time, and he realized that different forms of life had been alive at different times in the history of the Earth. He also made the huge discovery that there was no life on Earth *at all* a very long time ago.

Cuvier was one of the first people to realize that many kinds of living things that used to exist on Earth are no longer here, that is they have become extinct.

Catastrophic causes?

Cuvier thought that the reason why the fossils were different in different layers of rock was that God had sent a series of catastrophes. Each disaster wiped out many living things, and then new living things were created by God to fill the gaps, or moved in from other places where there had been no catastrophe. This idea became quite popular among religious people at the time, who thought that the flood described in the Bible was just the latest of these catastrophes.

terrible lizards

But whatever the reason, by the time Cuvier died of cholera in 1832, people had begun to unearth some really impressive fossil remains. These showed that the Earth had once been stalked by creatures so fierce that palaeontologists gave them the name 'terrible lizards' – or, in Latin, *dinosaurs*.

Mary Anning

one of the most well-known names in fossil hunting is that of a poor, uneducated woman who eventually became one of the most respected fossilists of her time.

The fossil family

Mary Anning was born in Dorset in south-west England in 1799 to a very poor family. Because they lived at Lyme Regis, where the cliffs are crumbling away and exposing fossils all the time, her carpenter father managed to make a little extra money by gathering these curious objects up, and selling them to fossil collectors.

Fossils were a serious business for the Annings. Mary would go out every day with her mother and her brother to collect them, and when her father died in 1810, this was the only way Mary, her mother and brother, Joseph, could make a living.

> **Lightning strike**
> There is a strange story that when Mary Anning was about a year old, a girl who had been carrying her along the beach was struck by lightning and killed. Mary was not expected to live. But she swiftly recovered and was thought by her parents to be much more alert than she ever had been before the lightning strike.

A big find

In 1811, fifteen-year-old Joseph found the large fossilized head of a terrifying looking creature, with rows of razor-sharp teeth, exposed in the cliffs. Mary, who was still only twelve, carefully dug away at the soft chalk to expose the complete skeleton of the creature, which looked rather like an enormous crocodile. It was named *Ichthyosaurus* in 1817 – the first ichthyosaur ever discovered.

The fossil was so rare and impressive that the delighted family were able to sell it to a rich collector for £23 – a princely sum in those days.

While Joseph went on to get a secure job as a furniture upholsterer, Mary carried on the fossil-collecting business. She was really good at digging them out of the soft rock without damaging them. Despite her lack of education, she was fascinated by her finds and read everything she could about geology and palaeontology.

The tongue twister, 'She sells seashells on the seashore,' refers to Mary Anning selling her fossil specimens.

She sells seashells . . .

Sadly, because she was a girl, there was no way Mary could get any financial help to further her education. At this time women weren't even allowed to join organizations like the Royal Society. Instead, she worked very hard at her collecting. The best time to find fossils was in the worst weather, when the rain and waves crumbled the cliffs away. Mary would be out scouring the rocks in the soaking wet, wearing an old top hat, a cloak and as many skirts as she could find just to keep out the cold. A good find could make enough money to feed the family for a week, and a spectacular one for far longer.

Despite her poverty and poor education, Mary Anning was eventually known by reputation as 'the most eminent woman fossilist'.

Mary versus the gentlemen scientists

Mary studied her finds by comparing their bone structure with creatures that were still alive. She actually became more knowledgeable than many of the highly educated men who bought her fossils. Gentlemen fossil hunters would visit her in Dorset and pick her brains. Then they would be the ones to name the new species she had found and to get the glory by writing up the discovery – Mary would never get a mention. When her ichthyosaur find was published she wasn't even sent a copy.

This would be disgraceful behaviour today but attitudes towards women were very different then, and this was perfectly acceptable at that time. Some of her clients were kinder than others, though. When palaeontologist Thomas Birch found that the family was in desperate need of money, he sold the fossil ichthyosaur that he had bought from Mary for a higher price, and sent the money to her family.

A major discovery

In the winter of 1821, Mary discovered and excavated an almost complete fossil skeleton of an incredible creature. There was no skull but the 1.5 metre animal had a long neck and tail, paddle-like limbs ending in five digits (like fingers or toes), and plates of bone (rather like armour) covering its middle.

Mary had to move the entire skeleton bone by bone, but she forgot which bone had linked to which, making it difficult to reconstruct it afterwards.

A stained-glass window in Lyme Regis Parish Church, paid for by the Geological Society, commemorates her '. . . usefulness in furthering the science of geology . . .'

Mary sold the skeleton to a Colonel Birch for £100. Birch invited his friend William Conybeare to study it and he gave it the name *Plesiosaur*, which means 'near reptile'.

Recognition

Eventually the establishment could not ignore Mary's incredible knowledge and practical skills as a palaeontologist, and thanks to the efforts of famous geologist William Buckland and the Geological Society, in the last years of her life Mary was given a small grant from the government to help with her work. When she died in 1847, her contribution to science was recognized by a eulogy (a speech given about her achievements) from the Geological Society, which was a rare honour. She is buried in Lyme Regis.

Mary Anning was the first person to discover dinosaurs that lived in the sea, but land-dwelling dinosaurs weren't discovered until 1822.

Gideon Mantell

The best palaeontologist of his day, this was a man obsessed with dinosaurs.

Doctor Dinosaur

Nearly ten years older than Mary Anning, Gideon Mantell was born in Lewes, Sussex, on 3 February 1790. Like Priestley, Mantell came from a Nonconformist background. Because of this, Gideon was educated at a Nonconformist school. He worked hard and ended up apprenticed to a doctor, becoming an expert in obstetrics (pregnancy and childbirth). He was much loved and respected around Lewes for his excellent medical care.

Mantell was a very caring man and there are many examples of him helping others in all sorts of ways, but his greatest passion was the study of fossils, which he found in local quarries.

There was a lot of road building going on in Sussex at the time, improving the routes to the increasingly popular seaside town of Brighton. Local quarries were extremely busy extracting stone to make the roads, and Gideon became friendly with some of the quarrymen who sold him all the fossils that they found. Mantell's wife, Mary Woodhouse, whom he married in 1816, shared his passion for fossil hunting and she made meticulous drawings of their finds. She must have been a patient woman – as Mantell's collection grew, he turned their front parlour into a museum to display his fossils!

At this time fourteen out of every 1,000 women died in childbirth, but out of the 2,400 births Mantell attended throughout his career, only two mothers died.

The fossils Mantell found came from strata dating to the Mesozoic era, 225 million to 65 million years ago.

Mary's monster

The Mantells' most spectacular discovery came in 1822. Mary spotted an unusually large fossilized tooth. They found more teeth and the bones of a fantastically large lizard-like creature. Mantell gave it the name *Iguanodon* and, despite its huge size, rightly deduced that it was a plant-eater and not a carnivore.

The iguanodon discovery was so important that Mantell was elected as a Fellow of the Royal Society the same year. A full-size model of an iguanodon was among the sculptures by Benjamin Hawkins Waterhouse made for the gardens of Crystal Palace when it was moved to South London.

Mantell's training as a surgeon was a great help in reconstructing fossil skeletons, because he had a good idea how bones joined together.

Dinosaurs, dinosaurs . . .

Mantell became obsessed with his dinosaurs. He found fossils of armoured carnivorous dinosaurs in 1832, and decided to give up his medical practice in Lewes and move to Brighton to spend all his time finding fossils, running his museum, giving lectures and writing. Unfortunately, without his income as a doctor, Mantell became increasingly short of money. He decided to rent out his house/museum and move into lodgings. The family split up and Mary and the children moved to a small rented cottage in Lewes. Despite their forced separation, Gideon and Mary remained on good terms and were devoted to their children.

On New Year's Eve 1853, twenty-two scientists dined in the stomach of the partially finished iguanodon sculpture to celebrate the finishing of the figures.

In 1838, Mantell sold his fossil collection to the British Museum, and in 1844 he moved to London. He died there in 1852, a year after seeing the iguanodon model pulling in the crowds at Crystal Palace.

Although he never had the benefit of wealth or a university education, Gideon Mantell was one of the best palaeontologists of his day. He wrote sixty-seven books, including *The Fossils of the South Downs*, published in 1822, and *The Wonders of Geology*, published in 1838. Just as important as his scientific discoveries, he also did much to make science popular and to fire the public imagination. But he didn't invent the name 'dinosaur'.

Richard Owen

the man who invented the name 'dinosaur'.

the dinosaur man

Richard Owen was only eighteen when Gideon and Mary Mantell discovered the iguanodon. Born in Lancaster, England, in July 1804, his father died when Richard was only five years old. His mother was just able to afford to send him to Lancaster Grammar School, but here Richard, who was clearly an intelligent boy, got into trouble for being 'lazy and impudent'. He thought that he knew better than all the teachers and therefore didn't need to work hard.

In later life, Richard would get a reputation for arrogance, particularly when it came to his ideas about the human brain.

from sailor to scientist

After finishing school, Owen did a spell in the navy but soon left to become a surgeon, eventually going to Edinburgh University in 1824. Here his arrogance surfaced again – he was dissatisfied with the teaching in the anatomy department, so enrolled himself in a private college instead.

Owen was a brilliant networker and in 1826, through his many contacts, he got himself a great job at the Royal College of Surgeons to help the curator, William Clift, catalogue the 13,000 animal and human anatomical specimens in the college's Hunterian Collection.

Owen fell in love with Clift's daughter, Caroline, but although Clift liked Owen, he insisted on the couple having an eight-year engagement!

The Hunterian Collection (named after surgeon John Hunter) consisted mainly of specimens that had originally been collected by Joseph Banks during his 1768–71 voyage to the Pacific with Captain Cook. Unfortunately, the previous caretaker of the collection, Sir Everard Home, had burnt most of John Hunter's notes to cover up that he had been publishing Hunter's work as his own. This left Owen with a huge task, having to catalogue all 13,000 exhibits from scratch.

Owen amazed everyone at Queen Victoria's court by telling them that tadpoles changed into frogs!

In 1836, when he was thirty-three, Richard Owen was made Hunterian Professor of Anatomy at the Royal College of Surgeons. Part of his work was to give public lectures. He was a really good speaker and his lectures became very popular. The ones he gave at the college and the Royal Institution became a famous feature of London life. Charles Dickens and Charles Darwin went to hear him, and Queen Victoria herself asked him to teach natural history to her children.

A smelly hobby

Owen had an arrangement with the London Zoo to carry out post-mortems on any animals that died there. The major problem with this as far as Caroline was concerned, was that he would have dead elephants and rhinoceroses delivered to their London home, where he would dissect them in a back room, filling the house with appalling smells. Caroline made him smoke cigars all day to cover up the offensive pongs.

Through dissecting animals, Richard Owen developed his theory of *homology* in 1843. This idea is that even though a lion's paw, a human hand and a walrus flipper all look very different, they have very similar arrangements of muscles and bones and do much the same sort of thing.

Dinosaur!

Owen studied the new fossils sent to the Hunterian

Collection and he reported the first specimen of an unusual Jurassic fossil from Germany, which is now known as *Archaeopteryx* – a sort of early bird. He examined the large fossils found by Gideon Mantell and concluded that the iguanodon and others were not the fossilized remains of lizards, as had been thought, but a completely separate group of reptiles. In 1842, he grouped them together as *Dinosauria* (terrible lizards). Unfortunately, though, he used a lot of Mantell's work to create his dinosaur classification but never acknowledged it, so the two men became bitter rivals.

Archaeopteryx, found in Germany, looked like a small dinosaur but had feathers and hollow bones. At one point it was even thought to be a fake. It probably couldn't fly like a modern bird but could glide.

Owen and evolution

Like all scientists working in the mid nineteenth century, Richard Owen got caught up in the debate over evolution that followed the publication of Darwin's *On the Origin of Species* in 1859. Owen believed strongly that humans had souls and were therefore superior to and separate from animals. He dissected apes and stated that apes lacked part of the brain called the 'hippocampus minor'. He said this showed that human brains were unique and that humans and apes could not possibly have descended from a common ancestor.

Pig-headedly, Owen persisted with his argument even when another scientist Thomas Henry Huxley proved that actually apes do have a hippocampus – just like humans.

Owen seems to have been an arrogant man who could be jealous of the success of others and reluctant to acknowledge his own mistakes. But he did important work on dinosaurs and he also went on to be the first superintendent of what we now know as the Natural History Museum, London, overseeing the separation of the natural-history collections of the British Museum into a new and purpose-built museum. Owen died in 1892.

science evolves

By the time of Owen's death, Earth and life sciences were unrecognizable from the amateur gentlemen's studies at the beginning of the century. The way biologists thought about living things and the relationship to fossils had been completely transformed – by the theory of evolution by natural selection. Most people know that Charles Darwin came up with this idea. But while Darwin was still wondering whether he dared to publish his discovery, another brilliant scientist came up with exactly the same idea entirely independently. His name was Alfred Russel Wallace.

Evolve
or
Die

Evolve or Die

In the nineteenth century, an exciting new theory would change forever our view of life on Earth. Everybody knows that Charles Darwin was one of the discoverers of evolution by natural selection but few people know that it was also discovered by Alfred Russel Wallace. The final piece of the evolutionary puzzle was put into place by a clever but unknown monk.

Alfred Russel Wallace

A man who thrived on exciting expeditions, he had the famous realization that '. . . only the fittest will survive'.

Alfred was very upset when his mother made him wear black sleeves over the arms of his school-uniform jacket to protect it (they were too poor to buy him a new one). Other children laughed at him and he felt humiliated. When he grew up he was always very careful to show respect to others and never to put them in humiliating situations.

For richer, for poorer

Alfred was born in Wales in 1823, one of eight children. His family were reasonably well off when he was born but gradually got poorer as his father invested money unwisely over the years. By the time Alfred grew up there would be no money left for him to go to university and he would have to make his way in the world as best he could.

When Alfred was three, the family moved to Hertfordshire where they found themselves short of money and living in cramped and disease-ridden housing. Alfred caught scarlet fever, which nearly killed him, but luckily he eventually recovered.

Although Alfred did go to school, he had to leave to go to work in 1837, when he was fourteen, and was eventually apprenticed to his elder brother,

William, a surveyor, living with him in lodgings near Regent's Park in London.

For the next six years, the two of them travelled wherever there was work, just as William Smith had done in his days as a freelance surveyor. Also like Smith, Alfred became interested in the fossils that he saw.

Alfred had a strong sense of social justice. In his work he saw the hardship created by rich landowners, who enclosed their land so that ordinary people could no longer graze their animals on it. He described this as 'legalized robbery'.

The two brothers barely scraped a living but Alfred loved the open-air life and the opportunity to learn about the world. He was particularly interested in geology and botany, and read as many books on these subjects as he could lay his hands on. One of his favourite books was Charles Darwin's *Voyage of the Beagle*, which was published in 1839 and described what Darwin had seen on his famous voyage round the world.

Charles Darwin came from a rich family and had all the benefits Wallace missed out on. He was educated at Cambridge University and travelled around the world as a naturalist on board the Royal Navy ship HMS Beagle.

An influential book

William's surveying business was not going well and couldn't support both brothers, so Alfred found himself a job as a schoolmaster in Leicester. He wasn't cut out for teaching but at least it gave him time for his natural-history studies and to meet up with his new friend, amateur naturalist Henry Bates. It was around this time that he read a book that left a deep impression on him – Essay on the Principle of Population by Thomas Malthus, a book that also set Darwin thinking.

The struggle for survival

The important thing about this book was that it

showed how natural populations of animals are limited by things such as disease, famine and predators. Put simply, to keep the same size of population, each pair of animals in that population should have only two offspring who survive to grow up and reproduce in their turn. But because in real life many young animals die before they can grow up and breed, in fact, many more than two young are normally born to any pair of animals to ensure that at least two survive.

The message Wallace got from the book is that in nature there is a struggle for survival, and only a few individuals survive long enough to breed. The idea stuck in his mind but it would be years before he realized the implications.

A daring plan

In 1845, Alfred's life changed again. His brother William died, and so Alfred gave up teaching and took on his surveying business, based in Neath, South Wales. His old friend Henry Bates visited him there and their interest in botany and natural history continued to flourish.

In 1848, Wallace hatched an exciting plan to change his life once and for all. He and Bates would scrape together enough money to go to South America, most of which was unexplored. There they would make a living, and perhaps even become famous, by sending specimens of exotic plants and insects back to collectors in England. With barely enough to cover their travel expenses, the two adventurous young men sailed for Brazil in April 1848. Wallace was twenty-five, his friend just twenty-three.

Living in the rainforest was difficult and, at times, dangerous. Despite this, Wallace did a lot of exploring

Wallace stayed in Brazil for four years. He had enough adventures there to fill a whole book; on his return he wrote Travels on the Amazon, *which tells of some of his escapades.*

on his own, with only native guides to accompany him. He travelled into the jungle up the Amazon and the Rio Negro by canoe, and found dozens of species of plants and animals that were unknown back in England. He shipped enough of them back to make a little money and to gain a growing reputation as a naturalist.

Wallace came close to death on several occasions. Once, he left a loaded shotgun in the bottom of the canoe, which went off accidentally. It just missed him but the bullet badly grazed his wrist. Then Wallace caught malaria, which was very serious. Even worse, when his younger brother Herbert came out to join him for an adventure, he caught yellow fever and died. Alfred never really got over it and always blamed himself for Herbert's death.

crisis at sea

But the biggest adventure came on Wallace's voyage home in 1852. His ship caught fire and had to be abandoned. Wallace and the crew were left in open boats with just a handful of things they had grabbed before the ship went down. They spent a worrying ten days at sea before they were rescued by a passing ship. Wallace was lucky to escape with his life but sadly all his specimens were now at the bottom of the ocean and he had to return to England empty-handed.

Wallace had only been in England for sixteen months (during which time he wrote his book) when he started planning another expedition, this time to the Far East. He needed to make contact with people who would buy specimens from this trip. One of these prospective customers was the naturalist Charles Darwin.

Bates fared better, returning from South America in 1855 with his collections intact. Luckily Wallace had insured his collections, so did get some compensation for his loss.

Darwin and Wallace

By 1852 Darwin was forty-three years old, fourteen years older than Wallace, and had settled down to a quiet life with his family in Kent. He had spent the years since he came back from his voyage thinking about what he had seen, making natural-history observations and doing various breeding experiments, particularly with pigeons. All this was leading up to him developing his theory of evolution by natural selection. But he hadn't published any of his ideas.

Further travels

Wallace set off on his next expedition in 1854. By now, he had a reputation as a naturalist, so the Royal Geographical Society helped him get a passage to the Far East on a ship. He even had his own assistant, sixteen-year-old Charles Allen.

Wallace stayed in the Far East until 1862, and had many more adventures of the kind he had experienced in South America. He also had his big idea about evolution.

Evolving world

By this time scientists had realized that life on Earth evolves. Fossil evidence showed how species change as time passes, and studies by scientists such as Cuvier showed that different species are related to one another. Scientists were beginning to realize that, in fact, different species were descended from common ancestors. The question was, *how* did new species arise? Wallace had been thinking about this for years.

In a paper that he wrote in 1855, he described the variety of living things on Earth as being like the tips of the branching twigs of a huge bush. Everything had emerged from one single trunk, so everything was related to everything else. Species that were closely related, like foxes and wolves, were represented by twigs next to each other on the outside of the bush. Species that were less closely related, like wolves and whales, say, were represented by branches that were further apart.

If you imagine going down the twigs and towards the trunk as going backwards in time, that would mean the different species branched off from a common ancestor (a single twig). The fox and the wolf come from a common ancestor (twig) quite recently, but the branch that leads to the whale branched off much closer to the main trunk, which means dogs and whales had a common ancestor much longer ago.

survival of the fittest

One day, in 1858, the answer to the puzzle of evolution came to Wallace. He was ill in bed with malaria, dozing feverishly and thinking about evolution. Suddenly, inspiration hit him. He realized that the vital clue came from the population ideas of Thomas Malthus that he had read years before. Only a few individuals in each generation survive and have offspring. But the ones who survived weren't just lucky, they survived because they were the *best* – the ones who had some kind of an edge over their brothers and sisters. If an individual could run faster, it would escape from predators more easily. If an individual were less prone to disease, it would be more likely to survive than one that got ill, and so on. If each individual passed on these characteristics to its own offspring, the species would not only survive but also evolve. In Wallace's own words, only the *fittest would survive.*

Survival of the fittest doesn't mean that the healthiest survive, although that helps. It means that the individuals best fitted or adapted to their environment and lifestyle survive.

Forcing Darwin's hand

As soon as he was well enough, Wallace wrote all his ideas down in a scientific paper. He sent it to Charles Darwin and asked him to read it and pass it on to one of the scientific organizations in London for publication.

Darwin was stunned. He had come up with exactly the same idea – now called natural selection – as the explanation for evolution years before. Darwin was fully aware that these ideas would upset a lot of people, not least his deeply religious wife and the Church authorities, because they went against Biblical teaching. But now somebody else had come up with the idea and was going to publish it.

A political solution

Neither Wallace nor Darwin were present at the reading of the joint paper. Wallace was still in the Far East and Darwin was at the funeral of his son, Charles.

Darwin didn't know what to do. But then his scientific friends came up with a plan to share the credit for the discovery. Without consulting Wallace, they took Darwin's version of natural selection and Wallace's version, and put them together to make a single scientific paper with both names on, which was presented to the Linnean Society (named after Linnaeus) in July 1858.

Wallace was such a nice man that he never objected to this. He was proud to be associated with Charles Darwin (who was already a famous scientist in 1858), and later on Wallace himself even referred to the idea of natural selection as 'Darwinian evolution'. Darwin realized that he had to publish all his researches properly and went on to write his great book, summarizing his own life's work, *On the*

Origin of Species by Means of Natural Selection, or the Preservation of Favoured Races in the Struggle for Life, and published in 1859. *Origin of Species* as it is better known, sold out on the first day of publication.

Back home

Wallace returned to England in 1862 and settled down, getting married and continuing his scientific work. The honours Wallace deserved came to him late in life. He was elected as a Fellow of the Royal Society only in 1893, and he received the Order of Merit in 1910, three years before he died at the age of ninety.

The Order of Merit is the highest honour in Britain, and is limited to twenty-four living holders at any one time.

Pass it on

By living so long, Wallace was able to learn something that Darwin, who died in 1882, never knew. They had both come up with the idea of natural selection but there was a missing piece of the jigsaw puzzle. No one quite understood exactly how characteristics are passed from parent to offspring. This is called 'heredity'.

The missing piece

The key to understanding inheritance had actually been discovered by an obscure scientist living in the middle of Europe. It was published in a journal hardly anybody read while the debate stirred by Darwin's book on evolution was raging.

Gregor Mendel

Years of careful work by a dedicated monk in a corner of Eastern Europe marked the dawn of the science of genetics.

His farmer father, Anton, was interested in fruit growing, and improved his small orchard by taking grafts from other trees. This early introduction to horticulture would be useful for Mendel's later work.

Gregor Mendel was born in Moravia in 1822. He was actually christened Johann but Gregor was the name he took when he became a novice monk in later years.

Johann was a clever boy and his parents worked very hard to send him to school. But when Johann was sixteen, his father was severely injured in an accident and had to give up farm work. Johann had to provide for himself, working as a tutor to younger children. All the work, combined with a poor diet, made him quite ill for a while. But despite this, he managed to complete his studies and, by the time he was eighteen, he was keen to go to university. However, the family's financial situation was now desperate. The only hope for him to carry on his education seemed to be to enter the priesthood. This was not quite the drastic solution it may sound, as it meant he could become a teacher and carry out some scientific studies in his spare time. But as it happened, things turned out better than he could have dreamt.

wise men

The monastery in Brünn (now Brno) was a wonderful place for Mendel. The abbot had virtually created a small university from the dozen or so monks of his community, and had encouraged them to develop artistic and scientific interests. The group included a botanist, an astronomer, a philosopher and a composer. In 1843, the abbot was on the lookout to add to his small band of wise men, and Mendel's physics teacher recommended him.

Mendel would never again have to worry about where the next meal was coming from, and would eventually be able to send financial help to his family. He settled in well at the monastery, studied hard and, in 1849, he was sent to teach at the gymnasium (secondary school) in Znaim. He loved teaching and did a great job at the school. In 1851, the abbot sent him to Vienna for a higher scientific training. He was now twenty-nine years old, and Vienna was one of the greatest universities in the world. Here, Mendel studied experimental physics, statistics and probability. After university he went on to teach physics and natural history at a Technical High School for fourteen years, and it was during this time that he did his famous experiments.

Mendel was so kind to his students that if one of them got a bad result in his exams he would give him an easier set of questions to answer, to improve his grades!

The Friar Tuck of science

Mendel was fascinated by the subject of heredity, and chose peas to experiment on, because they grew quickly and showed a wide range of natural variation. He undertook a painstaking and accurate series of experiments that lasted for seven years. This was a strictly part-time activity when he wasn't teaching or fulfilling his religious duties. All the space he had to work with was a small strip of the monastery garden (just thirty-five metres long and seven metres wide) and a greenhouse.

Peas and pods

Mendel chose his plants carefully, only using those that bred true and had seven easily identifiable characteristics, such as the colour and shape of the pod. He wanted to see how these characteristics were

Mendel wasn't tall and was a bit on the chubby side. With his jolly, friendly disposition, he looked rather like a kind of Friar Tuck in his monastic teacher's clothes.

passed down through the generations.

For this kind of experiment to have proper and meaningful results, Mendel would need to work with a large number of samples – in this case, a total of 28,000 plants. He studied each generation separately, so that he could follow the inheritance of characteristics cleanly from one generation to the next.

This was a labour of love. Each experiment took a year to complete, and Mendel had to fertilize every single plant by hand, brushing the pollen from one 'parent' on to the flowers of the other, and taking care not to let flowers get fertilized accidentally.

A bit of rough

In one set of experiments, Mendel took plants from a variety with smooth seeds and crossed them with plants from a variety with rough seeds. In the next generation of plants, all the seeds were smooth. At first sight, it looked as if roughness had disappeared, or been bred out. This was not the case. When he bred the smooth-seed 'children' they produced plants in which seventy-five per cent of the seeds were smooth and twenty-five per cent rough. Roughness had returned in the 'grandchildren' of the original plants.

Mendel then bred the 'grandchildren' and found that the roughness returned in a certain number of plants. He realized that there was something in a pea plant that determined its properties. That something would now be called a *gene*, and the property it determines (in this case, seed shape) we call a *characteristic*. Each plant carries two copies of the gene. In the original generation of this experiment, all the smooth-seed plants carried two copies of the same gene (SS), which specified the characteristic smoothness. Similarly, each of the plants with rough seeds had two copies of the gene for roughness (RR).

In the next generation, each plant inherits one version of the gene from each parent. So each plant has one gene for roughness, and one for smoothness (RS). But the seeds are not each half smooth and half rough because the gene for smoothness is *dominant*. So if a plant has the genes RS it will be smooth. The roughness gene is said to be *recessive*.

In the grandchildren generation, though, there is a greater variety of possibilities. A plant may inherit either of the two genes from either parent. The possible combinations are RR, RS, SR and SS. So one quarter of the plants will inherit the smooth gene from each parent, and one quarter will inherit the rough gene from each parent. These offspring will have smooth and rough seeds, respectively. The rest will inherit the smooth gene from one parent and the rough gene from the other parent. Once again, where there is a choice only the dominant smooth gene is expressed in the characteristic. So out of all the plants in the third generation, only the twenty-five per cent of seeds that inherit the roughness gene from both parents will actually be rough.

Blurring the evidence

Before Mendel, people thought that characteristics were somehow 'blended' from both parents. But Mendel's work showed that during sexual reproduction, inheritance works by taking *individual* characteristics from either parent. The reason this is not obvious in human beings is that there are so many genes expressing so many characteristics that the body you end up with is made up of thousands of characteristics inherited from your mother and thousands from your father. These blur together to give an impression of blending inheritance.

Lost research

Mendel's work showed us how characteristics are inherited. He didn't discover where the variability came from or why some peas were rough and some were smooth. That's all to do with the nature of DNA, the stuff genes are made of, and DNA wasn't understood until the 1950s. But it was still an exceedingly important and exciting discovery.

No one would have imagined that it was worth looking for great new discoveries in the humble publication of Proceedings of the Natural Science Society of Brünn*!*

The natural thing for a scientist to have done next would have been to publish his results in a scientific paper or book. Not Mendel the monk. He presented his discoveries to the Natural Science Society in Brünn but, unfortunately, the journal they were printed in was so obscure that the news of his work simply didn't reach scientists in the rest of Europe. If it had, Darwinians would have realized just how important it was.

The end of a scientific career

Mendel's scientific career was cut short when the abbot died early, in 1868. The monks had to elect a new abbot from among their number and the highly respected Mendel was the obvious choice. But although this was a big honour, his new duties left him little time for scientific research.

In his last years, Gregor's health suffered. He was overweight, had heart trouble, smoked up to twenty cigars a day and suffered from kidney problems. He died in his sleep, at 2 a.m. on 6 January 1884. His obituary from the monastery remembers him for his great kindness but it wouldn't take long for the world to remember him for his science.

Mendel rediscovered

Just five years after Mendel had died, the Dutch botanist Hugo de Vries (1848–1935) published a book with the unintelligible title *Intracellular Pangenesis*. In it he tried to explain Darwin's ideas about evolution in terms of how cells worked.

Over the next ten years or so, de Vries carried out many plant-breeding experiments similar to Mendel's, although he was unaware of Mendel's work at the time. He reached similar conclusions, and only came across Mendel's papers in 1899 when he was doing some research.

He must have made the discovery with very mixed feelings. On the one hand, here was confirmation that he was working along the right lines; on the other, he had been pipped to the post, much as Darwin had by Wallace! But he was an honourable man, and when he published his results in March 1900, he gave Mendel credit for his work.

It was indeed the missing link in the theory of evolution by natural selection, and Alfred Russel Wallace, by now an old man, must have read about it with great interest.

'Pangenesis' was a term invented by Darwin in which he tried (wrongly) to explain how hereditary material gets into reproductive cells. It eventually gave us the term 'gene'.

chapter twelve

Forecasts and Freezes

Forecasts and Freezes

> By the mid nineteenth century, weather forecasting was beginning to become a proper science, rather than an art. And people were starting to wonder about extremes of weather – in particular, the ice ages and why they happen.

Robert Fitzroy

> By a curious coincidence, the man who invented the weather forecast also had a connection with Charles Darwin and the birth of the theory of evolution by natural selection.

A blue-blooded boy

The British Navy was so powerful that even the sight of a Royal Navy ship flying its Union Jack was usually enough to stop any trouble. This was called 'showing the flag'.

FitzRoy came from an aristocratic family. One of his grandfathers was a duke, the other was an earl, and he was born in England in 1805, the year Nelson defeated the combined French and Spanish fleets at the Battle of Trafalgar. Perhaps that was an omen, because when he still wasn't quite thirteen years old, young Robert was sent off to the Royal Naval College in Portsmouth to become a sailor.

FitzRoy was a model student. He was such a swot that he came top of his class at college and was the first person to get 100 per cent in his lieutenant's exam, when he was still only nineteen. After college he served as a lieutenant on several ships. Now that the war with France and Spain was over, the old Spanish Empire, which included South America, fell apart, and there were new trading opportunities opening up. The British were keen to take advantage of this, and Royal Navy ships were sent all over the world to protect British merchant ships and trade interests.

FitzRoy's career went from strength to strength. His aristocratic background combined with his hard work meant that he was destined for great things. Soon an amazing career opportunity turned up.

FitzRoy's First Command

The navy was also involved in surveying areas with potential British commercial interest, and one of the most important surveys being carried out at that time was around the southern tip of South America, the notorious Cape Horn, where many ships were lost in huge storms. The survey was being carried out by two ships: HMS *Adventure*, captained by Philip Parker King, and a second ship HMS *Beagle*, which Robert was asked to command.

The original commander of HMS Beagle, Pringle Stokes, had got so depressed in the stormy desolate Cape Horn region that he had shot himself.

This was an incredibly important job for somebody who was only twenty-three. HMS *Beagle* was at the mercy of wind and weather in the stormiest waters in the world, and her captain was responsible not just for the ship but also for the safety of the sixty or seventy sailors who manned it.

Given the appalling conditions it's hardly surprising that FitzRoy began to take a keen interest in the weather. He learnt to tell when a storm was brewing from changes in the wind and clouds, and especially from changes in the pressure of the air, recorded on a barometer, which he always carried.

HMS Beagle was only a small ship, just ninety feet (thirty metres) long and less than twenty-five feet (just over eight metres) wide at her widest.

A gentleman companion

The expedition didn't return to England until 1830, and HMS *Beagle* was so worn out that she had to be

Captains had the power of life and death over their crews, since they were authorized to inflict the death penalty for serious crimes.

almost completely rebuilt before going back to the southern ocean over a year later. FitzRoy captained her again with many of the same crew. This time he decided that in order to keep himself sane and avoid the fate of Pringle Stokes, it would be a good idea to have another gentleman on board, somebody of his own social status he could talk to and share meals with. This made sense, because in those days the captain of a Royal Navy ship was almost like a god to his men. He had to have complete authority, so that all his commands would be obeyed instantly.

All this meant that FitzRoy couldn't be really friendly with anybody, not even his officers. But he didn't just want a mate he could chat to. He had been fascinated by the geology and wildlife of South America, and realized how valuable it would be for science to take along a naturalist to explore and study the region. The person who was eventually offered the position was a bright new Cambridge graduate called Charles Darwin. It proved a momentous choice.

Darwin was a gentleman from a wealthy family and could afford to pay his way. Socially, he was a good match for FitzRoy, and his knowledge of geology and natural history made him the perfect choice.

Darwin had the right connections to get him on the voyage. One of his Cambridge professors was a friend of the man in charge of naval surveying at the Admiralty – Admiral Francis Beaufort. He devised the Beaufort scale, which measures wind speed.

HMS *Beagle's* second voyage

The second HMS *Beagle* voyage lasted until October 1836. As well as surveying the coast of South America, the ship carried on right round the world before returning to England. The studies Darwin made, particularly in South America and the Galapagos Islands, off the coast of Ecuador, gave him the raw material he would use to work out his version of the theory of evolution by natural selection. But the end of the voyage left FitzRoy, who had been officially promoted to Captain in 1835, and was still only thirty years old, looking for something to do next.

After HMS Beagle

First of all FitzRoy got married, then he got stuck in to writing a huge book about HMS *Beagle*'s two voyages. Then, in 1841, he became an MP and was active in reforming maritime law. His undoubted diplomatic skills were rewarded in 1843 when he was made Governor of New Zealand, then a new British colony. It seemed like a dream job but it would not be a happy time for FitzRoy.

The man who saved New Zealand

The colony had no money, and there were few soldiers to help the governor to keep order. There was constant squabbling between the white settlers and the native Maori people. FitzRoy managed to avoid a massacre by honouring treaties made with the Maoris.

But although FitzRoy kept the colony going, he made many enemies among the colonists, and he was not given a chance to build on his success. He was recalled in 1845 and made a scapegoat for the failings of the colony. Despite this, history has remembered him more

Native peoples were often treated very badly by white settlers in places such as North America, Australia and New Zealand. FitzRoy's attitude was very unusual.

kindly as the man 'who saved New Zealand'.

A momentous voyage

FitzRoy returned home on the merchant ship *David Malcolm*. The captain was very careless about safety, and didn't even carry a barometer. One night, when the ship was anchored off South America in waters that FitzRoy knew well, he noticed that the pressure on his two private barometers was falling sharply. Even though it was a still and clear, moonlit night, FitzRoy knew the drop in pressure meant a storm was coming, and he was afraid the anchor wouldn't hold. The captain would have been happy to go to sleep, with his ship riding on the lightest anchor, but FitzRoy insisted that a heavier one was run out on a chain.

While the captain was sound asleep, FitzRoy watched the pressure falling further still on his barometers. He persuaded some crewmen to run out a second, heavier anchor, even though there was no sign of bad weather.

The storm FitzRoy had forecast hit at 2 a.m. Even with both anchors the ship still dragged across the bay, coming within a stone's throw of sharp granite rocks, but if it hadn't been for FitzRoy and his skill at weather forecasting, the entire ship would have been lost with all hands killed.

A new direction

It was a sign of things to come. Back in England, FitzRoy gave up his political career and went back to the navy but ill health forced him to resign in 1850. Luckily, he was still wealthy enough not to have to work. In 1851, he was elected a Fellow of the Royal Society. His wife died in 1852 but he married again two years later. The same year, the British government decided to set up a Meteorological Office specially to look at ways of understanding the weather at sea and improving the safety of ships. FitzRoy was chosen to be its first director.

His job was to collect statistics about the kind of weather that occurred in different parts of the ocean (especially the Atlantic) at different times of year, and produce tables so that mariners could find out what kind of winds and so on to expect along their route at any particular time of year. The last thing anyone expected him to invent was the weather forecast.

The first thing FitzRoy did was to set up a system of storm warnings. He organized simple weather-observation stations at different places round the

The telegraph was a new nationwide network of wires that could transmit messages instantly. Telegraph wires tended to follow railway lines and they transformed communications in the latter half of the nineteenth century.

FitzRoy's storm warnings were so successful that in 1862 the owners of Plymouth Docks complained that they were losing money because there were so few vessels requiring repair for storm damage.

FitzRoy also invented weather maps, which he called 'synoptic charts'. The name is still used today.

coast of Britain. These consisted of a barometer that FitzRoy had designed himself, a thermometer and a few other instruments. Observers sent their daily readings to FitzRoy in London using the new telegraph system. The system only worked because telegraph communications were virtually instant-aneous. If they'd had to rely on messages being sent by horse, it would have been too slow.

In London, FitzRoy and his assistants gathered all the information and applied the rules FitzRoy had learnt from his years at sea to work out if a storm was likely, and where it would hit. Then they used the telegraph to send warnings to ports in the affected areas. At the ports, special warning signals were hoisted, so that ships in harbour would know about the danger. The storm warnings were a huge success. They saved thousands of lives, because sailors would stay in harbour when storms were forecast.

The first weatherman

FitzRoy began to understand the patterns of the winds and weather around the British Isles. He got more ambitious and started to use the information to make weather forecasts for the whole country. Information came into the Meteorological Office in London every morning by telegram. Then the team worked frantically to put it all together, drawing charts and working out the weather patterns. They had to do all the calculations by hand. By 11 a.m., a forecast was ready to be sent out to *The Times* newspaper to be published in its second edition of the day. In the afternoon an improved forecast was sent out to go in the first edition of the next day's paper.

But weather is notoriously difficult to predict, and sometimes FitzRoy got it right, sometimes he got it wrong. That's hardly surprising – weather forecasters still sometimes get it wrong today, even with satellite observations and powerful computers to help them.

Queen Victoria had great faith in FitzRoy and often asked him for a forecast before she decided to cross the Solent to her house on the Isle of Wight.

pressure of work

FitzRoy came under attack for his wrong predictions but he just carried on working six days a week at his job, as well as writing a huge book, *The Weather Book*, which came out in 1862. He was literally working himself to death, and even though he wasn't yet sixty he looked like an old man. He was also going deaf, which upset him a lot.

Robert FitzRoy was recently commemorated when the shipping area Finisterre was renamed FitzRoy, in his honour.

FitzRoy's wife and doctors tried to get him to rest but he couldn't. Every time he felt a little better, he went back to the office and worked as hard as ever. Then he would collapse and have to rest. Eventually, it all got too much for him and on 30 April 1865, FitzRoy cut his own throat and died. A tragic end to a remarkable life.

Just at the time FitzRoy was coming to the end of his tether, in Scotland another scientist was tackling an even bigger puzzle than tomorrow's weather – trying to work out why ice ages happen.

James Croll

From a poor farmer's son to a renowned scientist, Croll spent much of his life wrestling with the puzzle of the ice ages.

A new idea

The idea of ice ages was still a new one in the middle of the nineteenth century. It was only when geologists began to demonstrate how old the Earth really is and how conditions on the Earth's surface have changed dramatically over the aeons, that the concept of an ice age became acceptable. The work of the Swiss naturalist Louis Agassiz in the 1830s finally convinced people that great ice sheets had once covered Europe and left their traces scoured into the rocks. But then the big question was, *Why had they happened?* And could they happen again? Step forward James Croll.

Farming the land

Croll's father had originally farmed a decent piece of land but was a victim of the enclosures. The landowner decided to put four small farms together to make one large farm. He allowed the family just a cottage and a couple of acres of land.

Croll was born in 1821 in a village on the banks of the River Tay, in Scotland. His father, David, found work as a stonemason, travelling from job to job, while his wife and sons farmed a small patch of land.

It was a hard life, and although James had a basic education he soon had to leave school and help out on the land. But at least he had learnt to read, and he read everything he could lay his hands on, but especially books about philosophy and science.

Croll learnt his science backwards. When he came across a scientific law, in order to understand it he had to look up the ideas the law was based on. Then, in order to understand that, he had to look up the ideas those ideas were based on – and so on. There was nobody to help him but he developed what he later described as 'a pretty tolerable knowledge' of physics by the time he was sixteen.

That was in 1837, the very year Louis Agassiz was astounding his colleagues in Switzerland with the ice age idea. But Croll knew nothing of that at the time. He was now old enough to leave home and make his own way in the world, and although his dearest wish was to go to university, he knew it was impossible.

From job to job

He tried being a millwright (the person who sets up mills and makes them work) but hated it, eventually chucking the job and going back to live with his parents, who can't have been overjoyed. He decided that what he really wanted to do was study algebra, so he did, while working as a carpenter part-time to help out with the family budget. Although he enjoyed carpentry, an old arm injury flared up and eventually he had to give it up.

Since he couldn't do physical work, Croll next tried his hand at being a tea merchant – that enterprise failed too but ever the optimist, Croll was sure that things would get better, if only he could find the right job. Eventually he came up with the brilliant idea of running a hotel, and chose one in the town of Blairgowrie. Here at last was a job that would give him plenty of time to read and think about science.

There was just one snag: Croll was a teetotaller

(he didn't drink alcohol). There were sixteen other hotels in Blairgowrie, and they all sold whisky. Croll's was the only one that didn't – it opened in 1852, and closed in 1853.

The next four years were the worst in Croll's life. The only work he could get was as a door-to-door insurance salesman, which he loathed. Then, in 1857, his wife, Isabelle, became seriously ill, and they had to move to Glasgow so her sisters could look after her.

The next year Croll finally got a job as a janitor at the Andersonian College and Museum in Glasgow. The pay was nothing to write home about but the job was easy (so he had plenty of time to think) and he was allowed to use the scientific library at the college. Even better, Croll's brother came to live with them, and as he didn't have a job of his own, he used to go to work with James and do some of the work for him.

An icy problem

Croll spent most of his time studying physics, and learnt so much that in 1861, when he was forty, he wrote a scientific paper about electricity, and got it published. Now there was no stopping him. He wrote more papers and got them published (although perhaps the people who saw the address of the Andersonian on the papers didn't realize they were written by the janitor!).

Croll's next big thing was ice ages. In 1864 he learnt of an idea that had been around for some time but had never been properly worked out, called the 'astronomical model of ice ages'. This said that changes in the balance of heat reaching the surface of the Earth in different seasons might cause ice ages.

Working out this idea became Croll's main focus for the rest of his life. He published many scientific papers about it, and eventually a book *Climate and Time*, in 1875. By then he had carved himself a reputation as a proper scientist and, in 1867, he had been given a job with the Geological Survey of Scotland. In 1876, a year after *Climate and Time* appeared, he was elected as a Fellow of the Royal Society, and also given an honorary degree by the University of St Andrews. Not bad for a poor crofter's son who had learnt everything on his own from books! He lived long enough to enjoy his achievements, and died in 1890 at the age of sixty-nine.

Ice ages are long cold periods in the Earth's history, when ice sheets extend far out from the poles. The latest ice age ended about 10,000 to 15,000 years ago.

Why do ice ages happen?
- Ice ages are caused by cold northern summers.
- Cold northern summers can occur when the balance between the seasons changes.
- The balance between the seasons changes because the Earth wobbles in its orbit.
- The astronomical model provides an explanation for why the balance of heat between the seasons changes.

Astronomical model of ice ages

The idea behind the astronomical model of ice ages is that although there are always seasons on Earth, the balance of heat between the seasons isn't always the same. In the northern hemisphere, sometimes

Most scientists today think that the world is now getting warmer unnaturally, because gases like carbon dioxide, which we make when we burn coal and oil, are trapping extra heat from the Sun and causing global warming.

summers are very hot and winters are very cold. Sometimes summers aren't so hot, and winters aren't so cold. But the total amount of heat reaching the Earth from the Sun over a whole year is always the same. You never naturally get cool summers and mild winters for hundreds of years in a row, or warm summers and very cold winters for hundreds of years in a row.

The seasons happen because the Earth leans over a bit in its orbit round the Sun. During a year, it always leans in the same direction. But because it is moving round the Sun, sometimes the tilt is towards the Sun and sometimes it is away from the Sun.

When the northern hemisphere is tilted towards the Sun, it is summer in the north and winter in the south. When the northern hemisphere is tilted away from the Sun, the seasons are reversed.

Tilts and wobbles

Very long ago, when dinosaurs thrived, the astronomical model of ice ages didn't apply. The geography of the planet was different then and the continents were not in the right place for the effect to work. In Croll's day, though, nobody knew this.

The balance between the seasons changes because the Earth wobbles a little in its orbit, and the orbit changes shape slightly over thousands of years. Sometimes the orbit is very nearly circular, and sometimes it is more elliptical (oval in shape). This is because of the way the gravity of the other planets affects it. Over thousands of years the tilt of the Earth also nods up and down a bit, and the direction of the tilt very slowly drifts round in a circle, like a wobbling spinning top. Adding all these effects together is what changes the pattern from very hot summers and very cold winters to cooler summers and milder winters, and back again.

Croll realized that ice ages happen when snow and ice spreads over the land masses in the northern hemisphere. In the southern hemisphere, Antarctica is always covered in ice. But in the north today, there is lots of spare land close enough to the Arctic where snow can settle and ice can spread when a new ice age begins.

A new ice age?

The question Croll tried to answer was, *Why should a new ice age begin?* He thought that one should start when the northern hemisphere winters were very cold, so that lots of snow would fall and be turned into ice. He worked out that there should have been an ice age that ended about 80,000 to 100,000 years ago.

When geologists worked out how to measure the ages of rocks, they found that he was exactly . . . wrong! Before about 100,000 years ago, the world had been quite warm, like it is now. Between about 100,000 years ago and 80,000 years ago, when Croll said it should be warming up, it had actually been plunging into an ice age. This ice age ended about 10,000 years ago, *exactly* the opposite of what Croll had thought. But in a way, he was right.

In order to make an ice age you need *cold* northern summers. Winters near the Arctic are always cold enough for snow to fall. To make the ice spread, you need summers that are cool enough for some of the snow to stick around without melting. If it does, it reflects away some of the Sun's heat, and makes the world even colder. The way to *end* an ice age is to have very hot summers, which melt the ice, and it doesn't matter if winters are still cold. But that doesn't mean Croll's idea wasn't important. He had the right idea about changes in the seasons causing ice ages. Once he realized that there were only two possibilities, he chose the wrong one but he was wrong in exactly the right way! He showed his successors what was really going on. Sometimes in science, being wrong can be almost as important as being right.

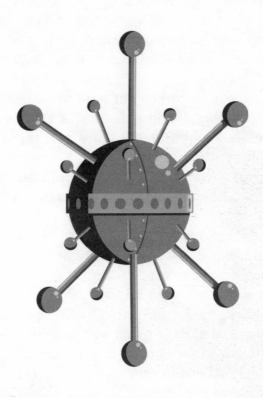

chapter thirteen

Bright

Sparks

Bright Sparks

The science that has changed our world the most is electricity. Without it there would be no electric light, no computers, no TV or radio, no phones - our modern world simply couldn't exist in its present form. The people who first discovered how electricity works would have been amazed to see how it has revolutionized our lives.

A natural phenomenon

Of course, we didn't invent electricity. It has always existed. Natural electricity makes lightning, and it is also at work inside atoms and molecules. But in spite of the pioneering efforts of William Gilbert in the sixteenth century, it is only since the nineteenth century that people have begun to understand electricity, and learnt how to use it.

In the 1790s, two Italian scientists - Galvani and Volta - first got to grips with electricity.

Leap, frog!

The end of the eighteenth century was a much better time for science in Italy. The Roman Catholic Church was not as powerful as it had been when it persecuted Galileo, and there was a lot of good work being done once again. One of Italy's new scientists was Luigi Galvani (1737–98), who worked at the University of Bologna. One day, as he was preparing some frogs' legs to be dissected by his students, he noticed that when a leg hanging from a brass hook touched a nearby iron grid, it twitched as if it were still alive.

Galvani thought that the movement was caused by electricity being made in the muscles of the frog but the professor of physics at Pavia University, Alessandro Volta (1745–1827), disagreed. He accepted that the movement was due to electricity, but he thought that it was being made when the two different metals, brass and iron, touched one another. He did experiments with lots of pairs of metals to prove this. Then, in 1799, came his big breakthrough – he invented a way to create electricity.

People were very impressed by Volta's invention, because it seemed to bring a force of nature (electricity) under control. When France's army took over the part of Italy where Volta lived, Napoleon made Volta a count.

Ever ready

Volta's invention was a pile of alternating silver and zinc discs, like coins, separated by cardboard discs soaked in brine (salty water). When the top of the pile was connected to the bottom of the pile by a wire, electricity flowed along the wire. At first, it was called a 'voltaic pile' – later it became known as a 'battery'.

Before its time

Although the scientific world was excited by the voltaic pile, it would be another twenty years before scientists used it to explore the links between electricity and magnetism. When they did, it would change the world forever. The most important of these scientists was another blacksmith's son, Michael Faraday, who worked at the Royal Institution in London.

Michael Faraday

Hard work and scientific brilliance enabled him to rise from bookbinder's apprentice to revered scientist. His discoveries quite literally changed our world.

A family of faith

Young Michael was born in 1791 (about the time that Volta was first noticing his electrically leaping frogs' legs) in a place called Newington Butts, which was then a quiet Surrey village but is now part of the busy Elephant and Castle district in London. Michael's father, James, was a blacksmith but he often couldn't work because he was ill. The family – Michael also had a brother and two sisters – were at times desperately poor but they had a very strong religious faith, which helped them to cope with the hardships of their life.

What a bind

Not surprisingly, Michael's education was pretty basic, and by the time he was fourteen he was already at work, apprenticed to a local bookseller and bookbinder. Michael learnt his trade well. The books that he made at this time still exist, and when he became a famous scientist he bound his own work into beautiful volumes.

But better than this, his boss, a man named George Ribeau, was very kind to his young workers and let Michael read the books that he had in stock. Over his seven-year apprenticeship Faraday read many books and developed a passionate interest in science, particularly chemistry. He even rebound a huge four-volume introduction to chemistry, interleaved with extra blank pages for his meticulous notes.

A turning point

Michael's life changed when a copy of the *Encyclopædia Britannica* came into the shop for binding. Faraday read an article in it about electricity, which really fired his imagination. He did all sorts of experiments, building apparatus out of any odd bits and pieces that he could lay his hands on.

Hoping to meet some like-minded young people, he also joined the City Philosophical Society, a group that met each week to hear lectures on science and discuss all sorts of scientific issues.

A stroke of luck

Faraday's boss was very proud of his clever apprentice, and one day he showed one of his most important customers, William Dance, one of Faraday's beautiful books, full of his notes and experiments. Dance was impressed and gave Faraday tickets to hear Humphry Davy lecture at the Royal Institution.

Faraday was enthralled by the lectures. He made detailed notes and drawings of Davy's experiments and, by way of thanks to Mr Dance, he bound them all together into a beautiful book and presented it to him. Dance was not going to forget this young man in a hurry.

Dreams and disappointments

Faraday desperately wanted to make a career in science but without a university education this

Unusually for this time, when women weren't even allowed to go to university, this lively group also included women on equal terms.

Sir Humphry Davy was one of the most famous scientists of the day. He invented a miner's lamp, among other things, and would one day become President of the Royal Society.

seemed impossible. In 1812, when he was twenty-one, his apprenticeship ended and he got a job with another bookbinder, who was nothing like as encouraging as Ribeau. Faraday hated working for him and spent every spare moment writing to prominent scientists to ask for work. He even wrote to the president of the Royal Society himself, the mighty Sir Joseph Banks. Sir Joseph never replied and Faraday was offered nothing.

Opportunity knocks

But then his hard work finally paid off. When Humphry Davy was temporarily blinded (by a particularly explosive experiment), Faraday's old contact, Mr Dance, recommended him as an assistant until he recovered his sight. Somehow, Faraday managed to get time off from the bookbinder to go and work for Davy for a few days a week. Once Davy could see clearly again, Faraday was forced to go back to his job but he made sure that he kept in touch with the great scientist. It was a good move. When the post of Chemical Assistant at the Royal Institution came up a few months later, Davy asked Faraday if he would be interested. Of course, he jumped at the chance.

In 1813, there had been a spectacular fight between the instrument maker and the chemical assistant in the main lecture theatre of the Royal Institution. The assistant was instantly dismissed and the job became vacant.

At last Faraday had a proper job in science. His salary was one guinea a week, plus candles and fuel and two rooms to live in at the Royal Institution – perfect!

Friends with the boss

Faraday was very skilled at making scientific apparatus and he became quite well known as a demonstrator for the famous Royal Institution lectures. He worked with Davy a lot, and they got on famously. When Davy got married, he even took Faraday along on his combined honeymoon and working tour of Europe so that the two men could study the chemistry of volcanic lavas. This caused some tension, particularly as Davy's new wife seemed to think that Faraday was there as their servant! Faraday kept quiet and made the best of it.

World of wonders

The party visited Paris, Italy, Switzerland and Germany. Faraday saw waterspouts and volcanoes, the telescope that Galileo had used to discover the moons of Jupiter and met some heroes of science: André Ampère in Paris and Alessandro Volta in Italy. For a man who had been brought up in two rooms with little formal education, it was an almost miraculous experience.

He learnt to read and speak both French and Italian, and returned to his job at the Royal Institution even more enthusiastic than before. He carried on assisting Davy, and in 1816–7, helped him develop his famous miners' safety lamp, which saved many miners' lives.

Life is good

1821 was a very happy year for Michael Faraday. On 21 May he was promoted to Superintendent at the Royal Institution, and his salary went up to thirty shillings a week. He was given nicer rooms and married Sarah Barnard, a member of his religious group. 1821 was also the year Faraday made some important scientific breakthroughs.

In 1820, a Danish scientist Hans Christian Oersted had discovered the first link between electricity and magnetism. He found that a magnetic

Faraday particularly enjoyed helping Davy with experiments involving nitrogen chloride – a highly reactive chemical – because they produced a great many explosions.

The electrical units 'amp' and 'volt' are named after Ampère and Volta.

The 'Davy lamp' indicated when dangerous methane or carbon dioxide gases were present in coalmines and, unlike ordinary candles, didn't ignite the highly flammable methane.

compass needle brought near to a wire carrying an electric current would always move in a certain direction. This suggested that the magnetic force was acting in a circle round the wire. This was such an intriguing idea that scientists all over Europe started to experiment with the new 'electromagnetism'. Faraday wasn't to be left out. His experiments proved that a changing electric field (such as the one made by a moving electric current) created a magnetic field. This is the scientific principle behind the electric motor.

An unexpected reaction

In 1824, Faraday was up for election to become a Fellow of the Royal Society. Davy, once his friend and mentor, was the one person who voted against him.

Unfortunately, this caused a row with some other scientists who had been thinking along similar lines and didn't realize at first how original Faraday's work was. They thought he had used some of their ideas without acknowledging them. They were wrong but it still caused bad feeling.

Even Davy, who could never quite accept that his assistant had developed into a great scientist in his own right, felt that Faraday was somehow in the wrong, and, sadly, their friendship broke up.

Faraday's other work

Faraday was no mean chemist, either. In 1823 he became the first person to liquefy chlorine and in 1825 he discovered the chemical compound benzene. The same year, he was made Director of the laboratory at the Royal Institution.

He also introduced a series of weekly meetings at the Royal Institution (the Friday Evening Discourses) at which he often spoke himself, and in the late 1820s he started a series of Christmas lectures for children. This tradition continues to the present day – the Christmas lectures are given by a different guest lecturer each year and are broadcast on TV. Both have introduced generations of people to the wonders of science.

Another breakthrough

When Davy retired in 1827, Faraday became Professor of Chemistry at the Royal Institution and, like Davy, was even offered a knighthood. However, he turned it down because it was against his religious principles.

In 1831, ten years after the discovery of the principle of the electric motor, Faraday discovered that a changing magnetic field (such as the one made by whirling a magnet round in a circle) makes an electric field. This is called 'electromagnetic induction', the scientific principle behind the electric transformer and generator. Faraday's two discoveries in electromagnetism are the basis of the technology that powers our world.

Faraday continued to work on electricity throughout the 1830s, giving science the words 'anode', 'cathode', 'electrode', 'electrolyte' and 'ion'.

During the Crimean War, Faraday was asked by the Admiralty to devise ways of improving the quality of food used by the navy.

For the good of the people

Faraday's religious beliefs meant that he wanted to do good for people in his scientific work. Among his many achievements, he worked out ways of improving glass for navigational instruments, invented an improved chimney for the oil-burning lamps in

lighthouses (which worked so well it was used in Buckingham Palace) and he also advised mining companies and the government on mine safety.

A forceful idea

You can see lines of force round a bar magnet by putting it under a sheet of white paper and sprinkling iron filings on top of the paper.

Faraday sealed and dated the note and placed it in a safe at the Royal Society, to be opened after his death. Despite this, in 1846, he went ahead and let his ideas be known to the world.

We now know that light is electromagnetic radiation, and we can calculate the speed at which it travels.

Throughout his long life, Faraday never lost his fascination for electricity and magnetism. As early as 1831 he realized that magnetic forces didn't operate in straight lines, and described 'lines of force' that curve round a magnet.

He was also convinced that, as well as not acting in straight lines, the magnetic force might not be transmitted instantaneously but would take time to propagate through space. It would be many years before Faraday went public with these ideas, partly because of his other work and partly because it was such a revolutionary idea at the time.

In 1832, he wrote a note explaining his thoughts and comparing the movement of the magnetic force to the 'vibrations upon the surface of disturbed water, or those of air in the phenomena of sound: i.e. I am inclined to think the vibratory theory will apply to these phenomena, as it does to sound, and most probably to light.'

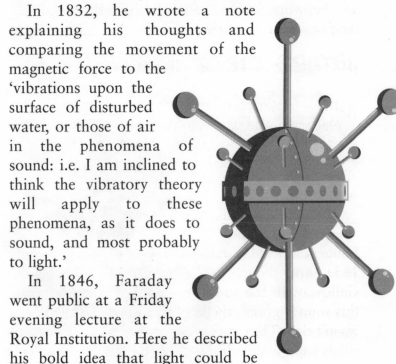

In 1846, Faraday went public at a Friday evening lecture at the Royal Institution. Here he described his bold idea that light could be explained as vibrations of electric and magnetic lines of force, reaching out from electric or magnetic objects like waves. He also suggested that light takes time to travel from one place to another and believed that gravity must act in a similar way.

It was this package of great ideas that Faraday passed on to the next generation of scientists, including James Clerk Maxwell, who was to build on Faraday's ideas and develop a complete wave theory of light.

A royal gift

Unlike many scientists, Faraday made his discoveries relatively late in life, and continued to do so well into his fifties. But he eventually retired from the Royal Institution and, in 1858, was given a house at Hampton Court by Queen Victoria in recognition of all the work he had done. He died there on 25 August 1867.

James Clerk Maxwell

The scientist who picked up on electromagnetism where Faraday left off, his pioneering work on colour later paved the way for colour TV.

Faraday's successor

James Clerk Maxwell was born in Edinburgh in 1831, and then brought up on a large estate in Galloway, in the south-west of Scotland. Although this sounds grand, the land was poor and the family wasn't rich. The estate was very isolated, because the roads were so dreadful in those days, and it was hard

James's father, John, was very interested in science and used to go to meetings of the Royal Society of Edinburgh. It would take an entire day just to get there.

to travel to other places.

James had a very happy childhood until he was eight. He didn't even have to go to school, because his mother taught him at home. But then she died of cancer, aged only forty-eight. As well as being upset at losing his mother, young James had to cope with an unpleasant tutor who his father hired for him. The tutor taught the boy virtually nothing, then beat him if he got things wrong. For two years James put up with it, as he didn't want to cause any more upset to his father. Eventually, John discovered what had been going on and sacked the tutor immediately. He wanted to do the best thing by James so he was sent to school at the Edinburgh Academy at the age of ten.

Not dressed to impress . . .

James's father had made the clothes and shoes himself. In Galloway, nobody cared much what you looked like but in the smart city of Edinburgh it was a different matter.

Poor James. He turned up for his first day at the rather smart Edinburgh Academy wearing strange-looking home-made clothes and shoes, and with a country accent so thick that the other boys found it hard to understand him. They promptly nicknamed him 'Dafty'.

The nickname stuck throughout Maxwell's time at school, even though he soon turned out to be much cleverer than average, and went on to become Scotland's greatest scientist. It just shows, you can't always judge somebody from their clothes or their accent.

But James must have been a survivor. After the first couple of days he started to get on with the other boys and made a few good close friends. But the highlights of his time at the academy were the days when his father used to visit Edinburgh (the railway had been built by then) and take James to scientific meetings. When he was twelve years old he even saw some of Faraday's discoveries demonstrated.

A shining student

At sixteen, James went to the University of Edinburgh. He was there for three years then went to Cambridge University, which was becoming one of the best places to study science in the whole world. Maxwell was a top student here. He graduated in 1854 and became a Fellow of Trinity – Isaac Newton's old college. He was still only twenty-three years old.

He also worked out how human eyes could be fooled into seeing all the colours of the rainbow just by using a mixture of three colours. Special cells in the human eye only recognize red, blue and green as separate colours. It's the brain that interprets the mixture of these three colours, enabling us to see the whole colour range. But Maxwell then took his theory a big step further – he invented colour photography.

the world in colour

Maxwell had been thinking about colour since his student days, and his crowning achievement was made in front of an audience that included Michael Faraday. In 1861, he proudly demonstrated the first colour photograph at the Royal Institution.

He took three photographs of the same piece of tartan ribbon through three different pieces of coloured glass called filters: one red, one blue and one green. The photographs were in black and white, on glass plates. Each plate had the pattern of

Maxwell wrote his important scientific paper about electromagnetism, called On Faraday's Lines of Force, *while he was at Trinity College.*

The original glass plates were kept carefully at the Royal Institution. In 1961, a hundred years after the original demonstration, the images were projected just the way Maxwell had done it – they worked perfectly!

Space probes don't send back full-colour images but three different black-and-white images, which are combined back on Earth to make the colour pictures.

light and shade corresponding to the view through one coloured filter but there was no colour in the photograph itself.

Then, the images on the three photographic plates were projected together on to the same screen, through three different projectors, so that they overlapped with each other exactly. The light from each plate went through the same colour of filter on its way to the screen that had been used when the photograph was taken. So each image had exactly the right shading of red, blue or green. Amazingly, the combined image, made only of red, green and blue light, showed all the colours of the tartan ribbon.

This trick of using just red, blue and green to make all the other colours is used in TV today. Tiny dots of these three colours make up a full-colour image on the screen.

Marriage and moves

In 1856, Maxwell became Professor of Natural Philosophy at Marischal College in Aberdeen. Here he married Katherine Mary Dewar. The couple never had any children but Katherine helped James in much of his scientific work.

Maxwell set up the Cavendish Laboratory, which opened in 1874, and became its first head.

In 1860, Maxwell caught smallpox but he recovered and moved on again, to become a professor at King's College in London. This was where he did his most important work on electromagnetism. But he became seriously ill again, and had to resign in 1866. He was still only thirty-five, and went back to Galloway, where he had inherited the family estate.

Nursed by Katherine, Maxwell recovered and settled down to a quiet life overseeing the farm and doing science. He wrote a great book, *Treatise on Electricity and Magnetism*, which was published in

1873, and he accepted the brand-new post of Cavendish Professor of Experimental Physics at the University of Cambridge in 1871.

But just eight years later, in 1879, he died of cancer. He was exactly the same age, forty-eight, that his mother had been when she died.

wave theory of light

Maxwell's greatest work, his theory of electro-magnetism, started out from Faraday's idea of lines of force but went much further. Faraday had never been able to work things out accurately mathematically but Maxwell, who was very good at maths, found that he could describe every single electrical and magnetic phenomenon known in a set of just four equations. These are now known as 'Maxwell's equations'.

The German physicist Heinrich Hertz (1857–94) carried out experiments in the 1880s that proved the existence of radio waves.

Remember that a changing magnetic field makes an electric field, and a changing electric field makes a magnetic field. That was what Faraday discovered. Maxwell's equations describe this in terms of waves. You can think of this as like ripples running down a stretched rope. Vertical (up and down) ripples might represent electricity, while horizontal (side to side) ripples represent magnetism. The electric ripples are always changing, because they are going up and down, so they make magnetic ripples. But the magnetic ripples are always changing as they go from side to side, so they make electric ripples – and so on. All you need is to put energy in, like your hand jiggling the end of the rope. This happens when things like electrons (electrically charged particles) move about in atoms.

The Speed of Light

Maxwell's equations include a number that tells you how fast the waves are moving. This number is usually written as c, short for 'constant', because the speed is always the same. Maxwell was very excited when he worked out the calculations and found that this number is the speed of light. He wrote that 'we have strong reason to conclude that light itself (including radiant heat and other radiations, if any) is an electromagnetic disturbance in the form of waves propagated through the electromagnetic field according to electromagnetic laws'.

This was a dramatic discovery, because there was nothing about light put into the equations. In a sense, they predicted the existence of light. And they predicted more. Maxwell realized that there must be electromagnetic waves with wavelengths longer than light, invisible to the human eye. These are now known as 'radio waves'.

The discovery of radio waves would change the world in ways Maxwell could never have imagined. When you watch TV, the waves that bring the signal to the antenna are obeying Maxwell's equations, and the colours on the screen are made by mixing red, green and blue in the way Maxwell pioneered.

He also played a part in working out the kinetic theory, which we have already mentioned. That was based on the idea of atoms, and it's time we explained how scientists decided that atoms are real.

chapter fourteen

The Biggest Idea

The Biggest Idea

The word 'atom' comes from the Greek word atomos, meaning 'indivisible'.

If electromagnetism is the piece of science that changed our world the most, then the idea of atoms is the most profound idea in science. It took scientists a long time to convince themselves that atoms are real. But once they did, they could explain the existence of almost everything around us.

The idea of atoms isn't new. Even some of the Ancient Greek philosophers wondered if everything in the world might be made of small, hard, indestructible particles. People like Gassendi and Galileo, in the seventeenth century, also thought about the possibility. But that's all they could do – think about it. At that time, there weren't any experiments they could do to test the idea. So it wasn't real science.

The idea of atoms began to become real science at the beginning of the nineteenth century, thanks to the work of John Dalton. But even then, it took about a hundred years for the idea to be finally proved right by experiments.

John Dalton

His fascination with the weather paved the way for his astonishing ideas about atoms.

Science takes off

Dalton was born in 1766 in the village of Eaglesfield, Cumbria, in the north-west of England. His life neatly spans the period when science really took off.

When he was born, there were only about 300 people in the whole world who we would now call scientists. When he died, in 1844, there were about 10,000. He saw the change from the days of gentlemen amateurs, like Robert Boyle and Henry Cavendish, to proper professional scientists like Michael Faraday.

Dalton came from a Quaker family. (Quakers are members of the Religious Society of Friends, a Christian movement devoted to peaceful principles.) His father worked as a weaver in one room of their cottage, and the whole family – John, his brother and sister, and their parents – slept in the only other room. John attended a Quaker school. Luckily for him, Quaker schools were very good and he learnt not just the classics (Latin and Greek) but subjects like mathematics as well.

Dalton was a star pupil at school, and an impressed local Quaker allowed the boy to use his library to read as much as he wanted.

Dalton was very interested in the weather and made daily meteorological observations from the age of twenty, until he died fifty-seven years later.

Taking over the teaching

But his time at school was short-lived. When he was twelve, John had to start earning his keep and he seemed destined to have to work as a farm labourer for the rest of his life. Then, in 1785, he and his brother got a lucky break. They were given the chance to take over a Quaker school in the busy town of Kendal, which had been run by one of their cousins. Alongside his teaching, John learnt more and more about science, and he began writing and giving lectures.

In 1793, he got a book about weather published and was offered a job as a teacher at a new college in Manchester. For the next six years he taught maths and 'natural philosophy' (science).

He was such a good teacher that after 1799 he was able to make enough money to live on as a private tutor, which gave him more time for his own experiments and to think about science.

colour blindness

Colour blindness became widely known as 'Daltonism'.

Dalton had realized that he could not see colours the way most people did, in particular, he could not tell the difference between what other people told him were two different colours – blue and pink. It turned out that his brother was the same. Dalton had discovered colour blindness. He gave a lecture about his discovery in Manchester in 1794, and became well known in the area, as well as further afield.

weighty atoms

The atomic theory that made Dalton even more famous sprang from his interest in the weather. He was curious about the way that air could absorb water vapour, with the water somehow fitting into gaps in the air, like water being soaked up by a sponge. We don't know exactly how he got from this idea to his atomic theory, because his notes have been lost. But by the early years of the nineteenth century, he had realized that each element must be made up of a different kind of atom, with empty spaces between the atoms.

Elements are pure substances that cannot be broken down by chemical processes. Oxygen is an element, and so is hydrogen, but water is not, because it is a combination of both hydrogen and oxygen.

The key new insight Dalton had was that the atoms of different elements have different weights. So all atoms of oxygen have the same weight as each other, and all atoms of hydrogen have the same weight as each other, but an oxygen atom has a different weight from a hydrogen atom. He even made the first ever list of atomic weights, estimated from chemical experiments.

DiPPicult to accept

Dalton presented these astonishing ideas in papers and lectures. Amazingly, he was still only twenty-seven. But his ideas were very hard for people to take on board. Essentially, he was saying that everything was made up of tiny particles with nothing at all between them. Where was the common sense in that?

Dalton wasn't too bothered that people didn't go overboard for his idea. He wrote a book about it (*A New System of Chemical Philosophy*, 1808), and having presented the idea to the world, left it at that. At home in Manchester he carried on with his meteorology and other scientific interests.

Dalton died in 1844, a much-respected scientist. His funeral in Manchester was attended by a procession of a hundred horse-drawn carriages.

Final recognition

But eventually the importance of Dalton's work was accepted where it really mattered – in the scientific community. In 1822, he was elected as a Fellow of the Royal Society, and in 1833, when he was in his late sixties, he was awarded a government pension in recognition of his achievements.

A weighty matter

scientists all over Europe were intrigued by the idea of atomic weights.

Dalton's idea began to be taken up by others as early as 1810. A Swedish chemist Jöns Berzelius (1779–1848) did some experiments to measure the combinations of elements in various compounds. Between 1810 and 1816 he studied more than 2,000 compounds and worked out the relative atomic weights of all the forty elements that were known at the time.

Relative values

Gases contract (get smaller) if you squeeze them, and expand if they get hot, so to make sure results were always standard, measurements had to be made at the same temperature and pressure.

There was no way to measure the exact weight of a single atom. But experiments could tell you their relative weights. For example, oxygen atoms are sixteen times heavier than hydrogen atoms. Hydrogen is the lightest element, with an atomic weight of 1. Oxygen, sixteen times heavier, has an atomic weight of 16.

Scientists all over Europe were fascinated by the new idea. A Frenchman Joseph Louis Gay-Lussac (1778–1850) studied the way gases combine. He would measure the volume (the amount of space they took up) of two different gases separately before combining them and measuring the volume of the combined gas that they produced. He did this with hydrogen and oxygen, which combine to make water vapour. He found that two volumes of hydrogen combined with one volume of oxygen produce two volumes of water vapour. In other words, he ended up with the same volume of water vapour as the volume of hydrogen he had started with.

Avogadro's big number

These ideas were picked up and developed in Italy by Amedeo Avogadro (1776–1856). He realized that equal volumes of gas at the same temperature and pressure contain the same number of molecules, whatever the molecules are. We now explain what is going on by saying that hydrogen atoms come in pairs, called molecules, as H_2. As it happens, so does oxygen, O_2. Water molecules each contain two hydrogen atoms and one oxygen atom, H_2O.

Two volumes of hydrogen contain twice as many molecules as one volume of oxygen, and when they combine they make the same number of molecules of water as there were molecules of hydrogen to start with.

$$2H_2 + O_2 = 2H_2O$$

It's a gas

Another Italian, Stanislao Cannizzaro, realized that this might be a way to measure the actual weights of atoms and molecules. Under standard conditions, you can choose a volume of gas that contains two grams of hydrogen. (It has to be two grams, not one, because each molecule in the gas has two atoms in it.) This much gas contains a certain number of molecules, which became known as 'Avogadro's number', or 'Avogadro's constant'. The same volume of oxygen gas at the same temperature and pressure contains Avogadro's number of oxygen molecules, so it weighs thirty-two grams (2 x 16) and so on. This volume is just over thirteen litres.

Cannizzaro realized that if there were some way of measuring Avogadro's number, you could work out the weight of each molecule by dividing this number into the weight of the whole volume of gas. There are actually lots of ways to calculate Avogadro's number.

One way was invented by Joseph Loschmidt (1821–95) in Austria in the 1860s. He realized that you could find out how much empty space there is between the molecules of a gas by turning it into a liquid, and comparing the volume of the liquid (with all the molecules touching each other) and the volume of the gas. The pressure of the gas, from the kinetic theory, depends on the number of molecules in the gas, and how far they travel between collisions. The amount of empty space tells you how far they travel between collisions, so once you measure the pressure you can work out Avogadro's number.

stanislao cannizzaro

An eventful life as a sicilian revolutionary didn't put a stop to cannizzaro's scientific work.

Fighting spain

At that time, Sicily, along with other parts of Italy, was ruled by Spain.

It's amazing that Cannizzaro had any time at all to spend on science, as he led a very exciting and dangerous life. He was born in Palermo, Sicily, on 13 July 1826, studied medicine and chemistry at various universities in Italy and then got caught up in Sicily's fight for independence.

By 1847, when Cannizzaro was working as a lab assistant at the University of Pisa, the Sicilians were fed up with being ruled by the Spanish, and wanted their independence. Cannizzaro went home to join the rebellion against Spain. The uprising failed and Cannizzaro managed to escape to France.

It was fortunate that Cannizzaro got to France, because he was condemned to death in his absence.

He got a job as an assistant to the professor of chemistry at the Natural History Museum in Paris but returned to Italy in 1851. In 1855, he became Professor of Chemistry at the University of Genoa.

It was here that he worked on Avogadro and Dalton's ideas explaining the differences between atoms and molecules, and working out how to use Avogadro's number to calculate atomic and molecular weights. He wrote about his ideas in a pamphlet, which he had printed in 1858 and sent to some of his friends.

The pamphlet included tables of atomic and molecular weights and it became one of the main topics of discussion at a big conference of chemists held at Karlsruhe, Germany, in 1860. Cannizzaro's ideas very soon became accepted, and pointed the way to a proper understanding of the nature of the chemical elements. But he was distracted from following the ideas up himself when violence flared up again.

Garibaldi was so successful that he went on to unite the whole of Italy and turn it into one country under King Victor Emmanuel II.

As well as his scientific work, Cannizzaro was a senator in the Italian Parliament from 1871, eventually becoming Vice President of the senate.

Garibaldi and the rebels

In 1860, Sicily rebelled again. This time they were led by a forty-three-year-old professional soldier Giuseppe Garibaldi, and once again Cannizzaro joined the ranks of the revolutionaries. The revolt was successful.

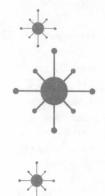

After the fighting in Sicily had finished, Cannizzaro became Professor of Chemistry at his hometown of Palermo. He then went to Rome to be Professor of Chemistry at the university, and also founded the Italian Institute of Chemistry. He died in Rome in 1910, two months short of his eighty-fourth birthday.

The periodic table

By the time he died, Cannizzaro's ideas about atomic and molecular weights had been used to develop one of the most important concepts in the whole of science, the periodic table of the elements. Several people picked up on Cannizzaro's work in the 1860s but the one who did most to develop this into the periodic table was a Russian – Dmitri Mendeleyev.

Dmitri Mendeleyev

This poor boy from Siberia became the most famous scientist that Russia has ever produced.

Siberia is a remote part of Russia. In those days, conditions were very harsh in Siberia – more like they had been in Western Europe a hundred, or even two hundred, years before.

Russia, then still a relatively backward farming society, needed new scientists in its attempts to become more modern.

A harsh start

If anything, Mendeleyev's life was more exciting than Cannizzaro's. He was born at the town of Tobol'sk, Siberia, in 1834, the youngest of fourteen brothers and sisters.

Dmitri's father, Ivan, went blind when Dmitri was still a baby, and could no longer work. Fortunately, Dmitri's mother, Marya, was a tough, stubborn woman. She set up a glass works to earn money and saw the older children grow up enough to be independent. Then, in 1847, Dmitri's father died, and a year later, when Dmitri was fourteen, the glass works burnt to the ground. But Marya was undaunted. She decided to take her youngest son to

St Petersburg, the capital of Russia in those days, and get him an education.

The social classes in Russia were very rigidly divided, and the people in St Petersburg looked down on people from remote areas like Siberia. Even though Dmitri had been very well educated at home, there was no hope of a poor boy from Siberia being allowed to study at the university. Instead, in 1850, when he was sixteen, he went to a teacher training college. Just ten weeks later, Marya died, leaving Dmitri alone in the world. But he seems to have inherited her indomitable spirit.

Talent recognized

Mendeleyev did well at college and was actually allowed to take a master's degree in chemistry at the University of St Petersburg. He graduated in 1856, and spent two years working at the university.

The government decided to pay for some of its best young scientists to study in the scientific centres of Europe, and Mendeleyev was chosen. He was sent to Paris and Heidelberg, and at the Karlsruhe meeting of 1860, he met Cannizzaro, getting a copy of his pamphlet on atomic and molecular weights.

When he got back to Russia in 1861, Mendeleyev's career took off, and within five years he was appointed Professor of Chemistry at the University of St Petersburg – the very same university that fifteen years earlier had been too snobbish to let a poor boy from Siberia in.

All this time, since his visit to Karlsruhe, Mendeleyev had been thinking about the importance

The choice of Mendeleyev would prove a good one. He soon did important work on the development of fertilizers and the petrochemical industry.

This is called a 'periodic' table of the elements, because the pattern repeats over and over again.

of atomic weights. Like some other chemists, Mendeleyev had realized that if you wrote out a list of the elements in order of increasing atomic weight, elements with similar chemical properties to one another are often sixteen places apart from each other on the list. For example, using modern measurements of the atomic weights, helium (atomic weight 4) behaves chemically very much like neon (atomic weight 20). Lithium (atomic weight 7) reacts chemically in much the same way as sodium (atomic weight 23). Oxygen (atomic weight 16) has similar properties to sulphur (atomic weight 32), and so on.

Table talk

Mendeleyev had the bright idea of writing out a table, a bit like a chessboard, with squares for each of the elements. The lightest elements were in the top left of the table, and the heaviest elements were in the bottom right. In the table, squares across the 'board' were filled with elements going up in atomic weight as you go from left to right, all with different properties from their neighbours. But the columns down the 'board' were filled with elements with similar properties to one another, so neon comes under helium, sodium comes under lithium, sulphur comes under oxygen, and so on.

Mendeleyev's table was a bit like a chessboard set up for a game but with a few pieces missing. Even if you had never seen a chessboard before, you could look at the pattern the pieces made, and work out the shapes of the missing pieces.

Filling in the gaps

But Mendeleyev didn't stop there. Sometimes, the elements in the columns didn't match the properties of the element above them but they did match those of the element one place above them but one column to the right. In those cases, Mendeleyev simply shifted the lower elements sideways, so that they were under the ones they resembled chemically.

In order to do this, he had to leave a few gaps in his table. He said that these gaps must belong to elements that had not yet been discovered. And, from the properties of the elements in the same column as the gap, he could predict what chemical properties those missing elements would have.

But Mendeleyev's idea was a bold leap of faith in the 1860s. By 1871, he had improved his table to include all of the sixty-three elements known at the time, and he had only three gaps. It was relatively easy for chemists to search for elements to fill those gaps, since they knew, thanks to Mendeleyev, just what they were looking for.

All three missing elements were found over the next fifteen years – gallium in 1875, scandium in 1879, and germanium in 1886. And all had exactly the properties Mendeleyev had predicted.

This was sensational stuff at the time, and it eventually led to the modern understanding of atoms in terms of little nuclei (made of protons and neutrons) surrounded by swirling clouds of electrons. Mendeleyev was the most famous scientist that Russia had ever produced. He died in 1907, a few days before his seventy-second birthday.

Into the twentieth century

Just in case anyone was still doubtful of the existence of atoms, two years before Mendeleyev died, a young German scientist working in Switzerland came up with a way of proving the reality of atoms. It is the only piece of twentieth-century science that we will describe in this book but we can't resist including it because it is such a neat idea, and because it was really a hangover from the nineteenth century. Besides, it nicely rounds off our story of science from Aristotle to atoms.

That young scientist was Albert Einstein.

Albert Einstein

The man who became the most famous scientist of the twentieth century.

A rotten student

Einstein became fascinated by science as a boy when he was given a magnetic compass and watched the seemingly magical way the little needle moved about.

Einstein was born in Bavaria in 1879, and later went to university in Zurich, Switzerland. Albert was a clever but lazy student, who didn't bother going to lectures and showed no respect for his teachers. There were only five people on the course, and one of them failed. Out of the other four, Einstein came bottom, and just scraped a pass for his degree in 1900. Because he had done so badly, he wasn't allowed to stay on at university to get a more advanced degree, and he ended up working for the Swiss Patent Office in Berne, while doing science in his spare time, and also, to be honest, when he should have been working.

Microscopic motion

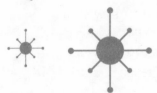

Einstein did so well working on his own that he was awarded a PhD by the University of Zurich for some work he published in 1905. He eventually went on to become a university professor and one of the most important scientists of all time. In a paper published in 1905, when he was still just a Patent Office assistant, Einstein wrote about a phenomenon called 'Brownian motion'.

Brownian motion was named after a Scottish botanist Robert Brown (1773–1858), who had studied pollen grains through a microscope in 1827. He noticed that the grains seemed to dance about, as if they were alive. But the same thing happens to tiny particles of smoke in the air, and they are definitely not alive.

In the 1860s, when Cannizzaro's work became widely known, some people wondered whether these tiny particles were being shifted about because they were being bombarded by atoms and molecules. But it seemed that that would mean the atoms and molecules had to be nearly as big as the pollen grains to do this, which was absurd. Then, Louis-Georges Gouy, in France, and William Ramsay, in England, guessed what was really happening.

Jerking about

They pointed out that if a particle in the air, or in water, is being bombarded from all sides by tiny atoms and molecules, sometimes, just by chance, there will be more atoms hitting one side of the particle than the other. So it will jerk away from them.

Robert Brown was also an expert on Australian plants, and was Sir Joseph Banks's librarian for many years.

Einstein is most famous for his formula, $E = mc^2$ – energy = mass x the speed of light squared. This essentially says that matter and energy are the same thing. But his work on atoms was just as groundbreaking.

Then, another side of the particle feels an extra push, and it jerks in a different direction. The jerks add up to make the particle zigzag about in Brownian motion.

Pinning down the numbers

Einstein's improvement on this idea was to show mathematically how the effect would arise from a constant but uneven bombardment by many tiny molecules, the size of the ones implied by Cannizzaro's work. But Einstein's biggest contribution to this was to put precise numbers into his calculations, describing the zigzag Brownian motion. He proved that although the particle follows

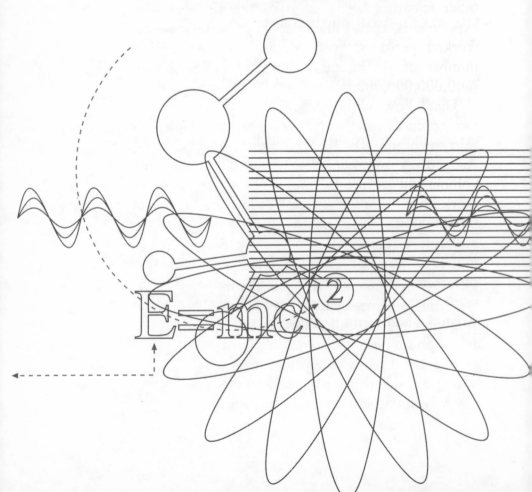

a zigzag course, and that the direction it will move in next is entirely random, the total distance it has moved since the first kick, measured in a straight line from the starting position, is always proportional to the square root of the time that has passed since the first kick. So the particle moves twice as far in four seconds as it does in one second, three times as far in nine seconds, and so on. This is true wherever you start measuring from.

How big is an atom?

Even better, Einstein found an equation that links the speed with which the particles move away from the starting point, to Avogadro's number. When other scientists began to test Einstein's idea with experiments, they found that his square-root rule worked perfectly, with a value for Avogadro's number of six hundred thousand billion billion (600,000,000,000,000,000,000,000, or 6×10^{23})!

That's how many molecules there are in thirty-two grams of oxygen. By measuring the volume of thirty-two grams of liquid oxygen and dividing by Avogadro's number, then converting the tiny volume you get into the radius of a sphere, you can work out that a single molecule is about 0.000000005 of a metre across. Each oxygen molecule is made of two oxygen atoms. So an individual atom of oxygen is about 0.0000000025 of a metre across, and other atoms are roughly the same size. Which would surely have amazed Aristotle, and seems a good place to end our story.

Index

A

acid, reacting with metal, 142
Agassiz, Louis, 208
air, 137
  air loss and burning, 142
  air resistance and falling items, 16–17, 73
  Boyle's law, 82
  'dephlogisticated air', 138, 139, 142, 146
  'fixed air', 133, 136, 137
  Greek ideas on, 13, 14
  molecules, 161
  vacuums, 83
  alchemy, 83
Alexander the Great, 13
Alhazen (Abu Ali al-Hasan ibn Al-Haitham), 22–4
amp, 221
anatomy, animal, 171–2
anatomy, human
  blood and it's circulation round the body, 50–52
  early dissections, 37–9, 40–41
  Greeks and, 19
animals
  Aristotle's study of, 17
  bodies adapting to lifestyle, 171–2
  classification of, 117–20
  experiments with, 83
  not having a soul, 57
  population sizes, 186
  survival of the fittest, 189–91
  Willughby's studies of, 114, 115
Anning, Mary, 173–6
apprenticeships, 86
archaeopteryx, 181
Archimedes, 7–9
Aristarchus of Samos, 31
Aristotle, 10, 12–13, 16, 17
arteries, 51
astrology, 62, 67
astronomy, 5–6
  comets, 105, 108–9
  distance from Earth to the Sun, 109–10
  eclipses of the Sun, 61
  Greek ideas on, 14–5
  Jupiter's moons, 74
  mapping stars, 104–5
  measuring position of stars and planets, 62
  planets' orbits, 15, 32–3, 67, 69–70, 99
  Sun moving round the Earth or Earth round the Sun debate, 14–5, 30–31, 32–3, 64–5, 71, 75–6
  supernovas, 63–4, 74
  telescopes, 74–5
  transit of Venus, 122
  Universe and the laws of physics, 47–8, 100
Aswan dam, 22
'atmospheric engines', 152
atoms, 84, 232, 243
  atomic weights, 234, 235–6, 237, 242–3
  Boyle's ideas on, 84
  and Brownian motion, 245–7
  Dalton's atomic theory, 234–5
  Greek ideas on, 84
  and heat, 161–2
  molecules, 236–7
  size, 247–8
'Auld Alliance', 132
Australia, discovery of, 123–4
Avogadro's number, 237, 247
Avogadro, Amedeo, 236

B

Babington, Humphrey, 96
Banks, Joseph, 120–25, 159, 168
Bates, Henry, 185, 186, 187
batteries, 217
Beagle, HMS, 201, 201–2
Beaufort, Admiral Francis, 202
Beaufort scale, 202
bees, 17
benzene, 222
Berzelius, Jöns, 235–6
binomial classification, 117–8
biology
  Aristotle and, 17
  Ray and Willughby and, 114
  see also animals
Black, Joseph, 132–4, 150
bleeding, 159
blood, 50–51
  circulation round the body, 51–52
  oxygen in, 160
bloodletting, 159